Poems 1968-1972

Books by Denise Levertov

Poetry

The Double Image
Here and Now
Overland to the Islands
With Eyes at the Back of Our Heads
The Jacob's Ladder
O Taste and See
The Sorrow Dance
Relearning the Alphabet
To Stay Alive
Footprints
The Freeing of the Dust
Life in the Forest
Collected Earlier Poems 1940–1960
Candles in Babylon
Poems 1960–1967
Oblique Prayers
Poems 1968–1972
Breathing the Water
A Door in the Hive
Evening Train
Sands of the Well

Prose

Poet in the World
Light Up the Cave
New & Selected Essays
Tesserae

Translations

Guillevic/Selected Poems
Joubert/Black Iris (Copper Canyon Press)

Denise Levertov
Poems 1968-1972

A NEW DIRECTIONS BOOK

Grateful acknowledgment is made to the editors and publishers of
magazines and anthologies in which some of the poems in this collec-
tion originally appeared: *Abraxas, The Amphora, Apple, Athanor,
Brown Bag, Caterpillar, Chelsea,* "Today's Poets" (*Chicago Tribune*),
*Citizen of the Imagination, Damascus Road, Dance Perspectives,
Decal Review, Descant, Earth's Daughters, El Corno Emplumado,
Field, Fubbalo, Hanging Loose, Intrepid, Journal for the Protection
of All Beings, Lillabulero, Madrona, The Malahat Review, Manroot,
Mill Mountain Review, The Movement Toward a New America, The
Nation, New American Review No. 6, New Directions 23, The North
American Review, Occident, Open Places, The Outsider, Partisan Re-
view, Poems from Summer Poems, Poetry, Poetry Review, Quarterly
Review of Literature, Quetzal, The Record, Red Clay Reader, Rogue
River Gorge, Rogue River Review, The Round Table, The Southern
Review, Stony Brook, Sumac, Up From Under, Voices from Earth.*

"An Interim," "Invocation," "Living with a Painting," the "Olga
Poems," and "Wings of a God" were first published in *Poetry.* "A
Tree Telling of Orpheus" was first published by the Black Sparrow
Press, Los Angeles, California. "A Marigold from North Vietnam" was
first published by Albondocani Press, New York. "Snail" was first
published by Cloud Marauder Press, Berkeley, California. "Wind
Song," "What Wild Dawns," "Secret Festival," "September Moon"
were first published in a pamphlet by Walter Hamady, Detroit, Michi-
gan. "Embroideries I" and "II" have been published by Black Spar-
row Press, Los Angeles, California. The quotation from Louis Mac-
Neice in the "Olga Poems" is from his *Solstices,* © 1961 by Louis
MacNeice. Reprinted by courtesy of Oxford University Press, Inc. The
quotation from Rainer Maria Rilke in "Life at War" is from *Letters
of Rainer Maria Rilke,* Volume Two, 1910–1926. Translated by Jane
Bannard Greene and M. D. Herter Norton. Copyright 1947, 1948 by
W. W. Norton & Company, Inc., New York, N.Y. Reprinted by per-
mission from the publisher. The quotation from José Yglesias in "Stay-
ing Alive" is from his *In the Fist of the Revolution,* copyright © 1968
by José Yglesias. Reprinted by permission from Pantheon Books, a
Division of Random House, Inc. The quotation from Vladimir Maya-
kovsky in "Staying Alive" is from his *How Are Verses Made?* (Gross-
man Publishers, New York), copyright © 1970 by G. M. Hyde. Re-
printed by permission from Jonathan Cape, Ltd.

Manufactured in the United States of America
New Directions Books are printed on acid-free paper.
First published clothbound and as New Directions Paperbook 629
in 1987
Published simultaneously in Canada by Penguin Books Canada Limited

Library of Congress Cataloging-in-Publication Data
Levertov, Denise, 1923–
    Poems 1968–1972.
    (A New Directions Book)
    Includes index.
    I. Title.
PS3562.E8876A6   1987   811'.54   86—5389
ISBN 0-8112-1004-9
ISBN 0-8112-1005-7 (pbk.)

New Directions Books are published for James Laughlin
by New Directions Publishing Corporation,
80 Eighth Avenue, New York 10011

SIXTH PRINTING

Contents

Certain poems which originally appeared in *The Sorrow Dance* and *Relearning the Alphabet* were later reprinted in *To Stay Alive* (1971). In the present volume, however, they will be found in *To Stay Alive* only, for reasons explained in the Author's Preface to that book—see page 105.

RELEARNING THE ALPHABET (1970)

ELEGIES

Dreamed the thong of my sandal broke.
Nothing to hold it to my foot.
How shall I walk?
     Barefoot?
The sharp stones, the dirt. I would
hobble.
And—
Where was I going?
Where was I going I can't
go to now, unless hurting?
Where am I standing, if I'm
to stand still now?

i

Twenty years, forty years, it's nothing.
Not a mirage; the blink
of an eyelid.

Life is nibbling us with little
lips, circling our knees, our
shoulders.
          What's the difference,
a kiss or a fin-caress. Only sometimes
the water reddens,
we ebb.

Birth, marriage, death, we've had them,
checked them off on our list,
and still stand here

tiptoe on the mud,
half-afloat,
water up to the neck.

It's a big pond.

ii

What do I know?
          Swing of the
          birch catkins,
          drift of
          watergrass,
          tufts of
          green on the
          trees,

6

(flowers, not leaves,
bearing intricately
little winged seeds
to fly in fall)
and whoever
I meet now,
on the path.
It's not enough.

iii

Biology and the computer—
the speaker implies
we're obsolescent,

we who grew up
towards utopias.

In this
amnesia of the heart
I'm wondering,

I almost believe him.
What do I know?
A poem, turn of the head,

some certainty
of mordant delight—
five notes, the return
of the All Day Bird—:

truces, for the new moon
or the spring solstice,
and at midnight the firing resumes,

far away.
It's not real.

7

We wanted
more of our life to live in us.
To imagine each other.

iv

Twenty years, forty years,
'to live in the present' was a utopia
moved towards

in tears, stumbling, falling,
getting up, going on—
and now the arrival,

the place of pilgrimage curiously
open, not, it turns out,
a circle of holy stones,

no altar, no
high peak,
no deep valley, the world's navel,

but a plain,
only green tree-flowers
thinly screening the dayglare

and without silence—
we hear the traffic, the highway's
only a stonesthrow away.

Is this the place?

v

This is not the place.
The spirit's left it.

8

Back to that mud my feet felt
when as a child I fell off a bridge
and almost drowned, but rising

found myself dreamily upright,
water sustaining me,
my hair watergrass.

vi

Fishes bare their teeth to our flesh.
The sky's drifting toward our mouths.
Forty years redden the spreading circles.
Blink of an eyelid,
nothing,
obsolete future—

vii

If I should find my poem is deathsongs.
If I find it has ended, when
I looked for the next step.

Not Spring is unreal to me,
I have the tree-flowers by heart.
Love, twenty years, forty years, my life,
        is unreal to me.
I love only the stranger
coming to meet me now
up the path that's pinpricked with
yellow fallen crumbs of pollen.

I who am not about to die,
I who carry my life about with me openly,
health excellent, step light, cheerful, hungry,

my starwheel rolls. Stops
on the point of sight.
Reduced to an eye
I forget what
            I
was.

Asking the cold spring
what if my poem is deathsongs.

At David's Grave

for B. and H. F.

Yes, he is here in this
open field, in sunlight, among
the few young trees set out
to modify the bare facts—

he's here, but only
because we are here.
When we go, he goes with us

to be your hands that never
do violence, your eyes
that wonder, your lives

that daily praise life
by living it, by laughter.

He is never alone here,
never cold in the field of graves.

11

While we were visiting David's grave
I saw at a little distance

a woman hurrying towards another grave
hands outstretched, stumbling

in her haste; who then
fell at the stone she made for

and lay sprawled upon it, sobbing,
sobbing and crying out to it.

She was neatly dressed in a pale coat
and seemed neither old nor young.

I couldn't see her face, and my friends
seemed not to know she was there.

Not to distress them, I said nothing.
But she was not an apparition.

And when we walked
back to the car in silence

I looked stealthily back and saw she rose
and quieted herself and began slowly

to back away from the grave.
Unlike David, who lives

in our lives, it seemed
whoever she mourned dwelt

there, in the field, under stone.
It seemed the woman

believed whom she loved heard her,
heard her wailing, observed

the nakedness of her anguish,
and would not speak.

The Gulf

(*During the Detroit Riots, 1967*)

Far from our garden at the edge of a gulf,
where we calm our nerves in the rain,

(scrabbling a little in earth to pull weeds
and make room for transplants—

dirt under the nails, it
hurts, almost, and yet feels good)

far from our world the heat's on.
Among the looters a boy of eleven

grabs from a florist's showcase (the *Times* says)
armfuls of gladioli, all he can carry,

and runs with them. What happens?
I see him

dart into a dark entry where there's no one
(the shots, the shouting, the glass smashing

heard dully as traffic is heard).
Breathless he halts to examine

the flesh of dream: he squeezes
the strong cold juicy stems, long as his legs,

tries the mild leafblades—they don't cut.
He presses his sweating face

into flower faces, scarlet and pink and purple,
white and blood red, smooth, cool—his heart is pounding.

14

But all at once an absence
makes itself known to him—it's like

a hole in the lungs,
life running out. They are without

perfume!
          Cheated, he drops them.
White men's flowers.

They rustle in falling,
lonely he stands there, the sheaves

cover his sneakered feet . . .
                    There's no place to go
with or without his prize.

Far away, in our garden he cannot imagine,
I'm watching to see if he picks up the flowers

at last or goes,
leaving them lie.

But nothing happens.
He stands there.

He goes on standing there,
useless knowledge in my mind's eye.

Nothing will move him.
We'll live out our lives

in our garden on the edge of a gulf,
and he in the hundred years' war ten heartbeats long

unchanging among the dead flowers,
no place to go.

15

i

Biafra.   Biafra.   Biafra.
Small stock of compassion
grown in us by the imagination
(when we would let it) and by
photos of napalmed children and by
the voice of Thich Nhat Hanh
has expended itself, saying
Vietnam, Vietnam: trying
to end that war.
                    Now we look sluggishly
at photos of children dying in Biafra: dully
accumulate overdue statistics: Massacre
of the Ibos: Do nothing: The poisoning
called 'getting used to'
has taken place: we are
the deads: no room
for love in us: what's left over
changes to bile, brims over: stain on the cushion:
And the news from Biafra (doesn't make the headlines,
not in today's paper at all)
doesn't even get in past our eyes.

ii

Biafra, Biafra, Biafra.
Hammering the word against my breast:
trying to make room for more knowledge
in my bonemarrow:
And all I see
is coarse faces grinning, painted by Bosch
on TV screen as Humphrey
gets nominated: then, flash,

patient sadness,
eyes in a skull: photo
of Biafran boy (age 5?)
            sitting down to die:
And know
no hope: Don't know
what to do: Do nothing:

At any moment the heart
breaks for nothing—

poor folk got up in their best,
rich ones trying, trying to please—

each touch and a new fissure appears,
such a network, I think of an old
china pie-plate
left too long in the oven.

If on the bloody muscle its namesake
patiently pumping in the thoracic cavity

each flick of fate incised itself,
who'd live long? —but this beats on

in the habit of minute response,
with no gift for the absolute.

Disasters
of history weigh on it, anguish

of mortality presses
in on its sides

but neither crush it to dust nor
split it apart. What

is under the cracked glaze?

Between waking and sleeping I saw my life
in the form of an egg made of colored stones,
half-made, yet the dome of it implied
by the built-up set and curve of the mosaic.
Star stones, lozenges, triangles, irregular pebbles,
brilliants and amber, granite and veined chips of
dark rock, glints of silver and fool's gold and gold;
and each was the sign of someone I had known,
                                    from whose life
of presence or word my soul's form,
egg of my being,
had taken its nourishment and grown.

Life yet unlived was space defined
by that base of uncountable, varied fragments,
each unique but all fitting close,
shining or somber, curve meeting curve, or angle
laid next to angle with unpredictable precision
—except in one place: and there a gap was,
a little hole, an emptiness
among the chips and flakes of spirit-stone.
It was a life missing that might have touched mine,
a person, Mathew Ready,
now never to be known, my soul-egg
always to be incomplete for lack of one
spark of sapphire gone from the world.

i

While the war drags on, always worse,
the soul dwindles sometimes to an ant
rapid upon a cracked surface;

lightly, grimly, incessantly
it skims the unfathomed clefts where despair
seethes hot and black.

ii

Children in the laundromat
waiting while their mothers fold sheets.
A five-year-old boy addresses
a four-year-old girl. 'When I say,
Do you want some gum? say *yes.*'
'Yes . . .' 'Wait!—Now:
Do you want some gum?'
'Yes!'   'Well yes means no,
so you can't have any.'
He chews. He pops a big, delicate bubble at her.

O language, virtue
of man, touchstone
worn down by what
gross friction . . .

             And,
' "It became necessary
to destroy the town to save it,"
a United States major said today.
He was talking about the decision
by allied commanders to bomb and shell the town
regardless of civilian casualties,
to rout the Vietcong.'

O language, mother of thought,
are you rejecting us as we reject you?

Language, coral island
accrued from human comprehensions,
human dreams,

you are eroded as war erodes us.

iii

To repossess our souls we fly
to the sea. To be reminded
of its immensity, and the immense sky
in which clouds move at leisure,
transforming their lives ceaselessly,
sternly, playfully.

*Today is the 65th day since de Courcy Squire, war-resister,
began her fast in jail. She is 18.*

And the sun
is warm bread, good to us, honest.
And the sand gives itself to our feet
or to our outstretched bodies,
hospitable, accommodating, its shells
unendingly at hand for our wonder.

*. . . arrested with 86 others Dec. 7. Her crime:
sitting down in front of a police wagon
momentarily preventing her friends from being
hauled to prison. Municipal Judge Heitzler
handed out 30-day suspended sentences to several others
accused of the same offense, but condemned
Miss Squire to 8 months in jail and fined her
$650. She had said in court 'I don't think there should be
roles like judge and defendant.'*

21

iv

Peace as grandeur. Energy
serene and noble. The waves
break on the packed sand,

butterflies take the cream o' the foam,
from time to time a palmtree lets fall
another dry branch, calmly.
                              The restlessness
of the sound of waves
transforms itself in its persistence
to that deep rest.
                    At fourteen
after measles my mother took me
to stay by the sea. In the austere presence

of Beachy Head we sat long hours
close to the tideline. She read aloud
from George Eliot, while I half-dozed
and played with pebbles. Or I read
to myself Richard Jefferies'
The Story of My Heart, which begins

in such majesty.
                 I was mean and grouchy
much of the time, but she forgave me,

and years later remembered
only the peace of that time.

The quiet there is
in listening.
              Peace could be

that grandeur, that dwelling
in majestic presence, attuned
to the great pulse.

The cocks crow all night
far and near. Hoarse with expectation.
And by day stumble red-eyed in the dust
where the heat flickers its lizard tongue.

In my dream the city
was half Berlin, half Chicago—
midwest German, Cincinnati perhaps,
where de Courcy Squire is.
There were many of us
jailed there, in moated fortresses—
five of them, with monosyllabic
guttural names. But by day
they led us through the streets,
dressed in our prisoners' robes—
smocks of brown holland—
and the people watched us pass
and waved to us, and gave us
serious smiles of hope.

Between us and the beach
a hundred yards of trees, bushes, buildings,
cut the breeze. But at the *verge*
of the salt flood, always
a steady wind, prevailing.

While we await your trial,
(and this is no dream) we are

free to come and go. To rise
from sleep and love and dreams about
ambiguous circumstance, and from
waking in darkness to cockcrow, and moving
deliberately (by keeping still) back into
morning sleep; to rise and float

into the blue day, the elaborate rustlings
of the palmtrees way overhead; to hover
with black butterflies at the lemon-blossom.
The sea awaits us; there are sweet oranges
on our plates; the city grayness has been
washed off our skins, we take pleasure
in each other's warmth of rosy brown.

vi

'Puerto Rico, Feb. 23, 1968.

        . . . Some people, friends sincerely
concerned for us but who don't seem to understand what
it's really all about, apparently feel sorry for us because
Mitch has been indicted. One letter this morning said,
shyly and abruptly, after talking about quite unrelated mat-
ters, "My heart aches for you." Those people don't under-
stand that however boring the trial will be in some ways,
and however much of a distraction, as it certainly is, from
the things one's nature would sooner be engaged with, yet
it's quite largely a kind of pleasure too, a relief, a satisfac-
tion of the need to confront the war-makers and, in the
process, do something to wake up the bystanders.
        . . . Mitch and the others have a great deal of support,
people who think of them as spokesmen; they have good
lawyers, and have had and will have a lot of publicity of the
kind one hopes will be useful—I don't mean useful for their
case, saving them from going to jail, I mean useful towards
clarifying the issues, stopping the draft, helping to end the
war.'

    But something like a cramp
    of fury begins to form

(in the blue day, in the sweetness
of life we float in, allowed
this interim before the trial)
a cramp of fury at the mild,
saddened people whose hearts ache
not for the crimes of war,
the unspeakable—of which, then,
I won't speak—
and not for de Courcy Squire's
solitary passion
                    but for us.

Denied visitors, even her parents;
confined to a locked cell without running water
or a toilet.
            On January 29th, the 53rd day of her fast,
Miss Squire was removed to a hospital.
All the doctors would do was inform her that
the fast may cause her permanent brain injury.

      'The sympathy of mild good folk,
      a kind of latex from their leaves;
      our inconvenience draws it out.

      The white of egg without the yolk,
      it soothes their conscience and relieves
      the irritations of their doubt.

. . . You see how it is—I am angry that they feel no outrage.
Their feeling flows in the wrong directions and at the wrong
intensity. And all I can bring forth out of my anger is a
few flippant rhymes. What I want to tell you—no, not you,
you understand it; what I want them to grasp is that though
I understand that Mitch may have to go to jail and that it
will be a hard time for him and for me, yet, because it's for

25

doing what we know we must do, that hardship is imaginable, encompassable, and a small thing in the face of the slaughter in Vietnam and the other slaughter that will come. And there is no certainty he will go to jail.'

And the great savage saints of outrage—
who have no lawyers,
who have no interim
in which to come and go,
for whom there is no world left—
their bodies rush upon the air in flames,
sparks fly, fragments of charred rag
spin in the whirlwind, a vacuum
where there used to be this monk or that,
Norman Morrison, Alice Hertz.

Maybe they are crazy. I know I could never
bring myself to injure my own flesh, deliberately.
And there are other models of behavior
to aspire to—A. J. Muste did not burn himself
but worked through a long life to make from outrage
islands of compassion others could build on.
Dennis Riordon, Bob Gilliam, how many others,
are alive and free in the jails. Their word is good,
language draws breath again in their *yes* and *no,*
true testimony of love and resistance.

But we need
the few who could bear no more,
who would try anything,
who would take the chance
that their deaths among the uncountable
masses of dead might be real to those who
don't dare imagine death.
Might burn through the veil that blinds
those who do not imagine the burned bodies
of other people's children.

We need them.
Brands that flare to show us
the dark we are in,
to keep us moving in it.

vii

To expand again, to plunge
our dryness into the unwearying source—

but not to forget.
Not to forget but to remember better.

We float in the blue day
darkly. We rest behind half-closed louvers,
the hot afternoon clouds up,
the palms hold still.

'I have a medical problem that can be cured'—
Miss Squire said last week when she was removed
from the city workhouse to Cincinnati General Hospital,
'I have a medical problem that can be cured
only by freedom.'

Puerto Rico, February–March, 1968

What wild dawns there were
    in our first years here
when we would run outdoors naked
to pee in the long grass behind the house
       and see over the hills such streamers,
       such banners of fire and blue (the blue
       that is Lilith to full day's honest Eve)—
What feathers of gold under the morning star
    we saw from dazed eyes before
stumbling back to bed chilled with dew
to sleep till the sun was high!

Now if we wake early
    we don't go outdoors—or I don't—
    and you if you do go
    rarely call me to see the day break.
I watch the dawn through glass: this year
       only cloudless flushes of light, paleness
       slowly turning to rose,
       and fading subdued.
We have not spoken of these tired
risings of the sun.

FOUR EMBROIDERIES

Rose Red's hair is brown as fur
and shines in firelight as she prepares
supper of honey and apples, curds and whey,
for the bear, and leaves it ready
on the hearth-stone.

Rose White's grey eyes
look into the dark forest.

Rose Red's cheeks are burning,
sign of her ardent, joyful
compassionate heart.
Rose White is pale,
turning away when she hears
the bear's paw on the latch.

When he enters, there is
frost on his fur,
he draws near to the fire
giving off sparks.

Rose White catches the scent of the forest,
of mushrooms, of rosin.

Together Rose Red and Rose White
sing to the bear;
it is a cradle song, a loom song,
a song about marriage, about
a pilgrimage to the mountains
long ago.
          Raised on an elbow,
the bear stretched on the hearth
nods and hums; soon he sighs
and puts down his head.

31

He sleeps; the Roses
bank the fire.
Sunk in the clouds of their feather bed
they prepare to dream.

Rose Red in a cave that smells of honey
dreams she is combing the fur of her cubs
with a golden comb.
Rose White is lying awake.

Rose White shall marry the bear's brother.
Shall he too
when the time is ripe,
step from the bear's hide?
Is that other, her bridegroom,
here in the room?

An Embroidery   (II)

(from Andrew Lang and H. J. Ford)

It was the name's music drew me first:
Catherine and her Destiny.
And some glow of red gold, of bronze,
I knew there—glint from the fire
      in a great hearth   awakening
the auburn light in her hair
      and in the heaped-up treasure
weighed in the balance.
              The events
were blent in this light,
out of sequence.

But always
there seemed a flaw in the tale as told.
If, as it said, she chose sorrow in youth,
what power would she have to welcome joy
      when it came at last to her worn hands,
      her body broken on Destiny's strange little wheel?
How could she take pleasure, when grief was a habit,
in the caprice of a cruel King's making her Queen?
And my Catherine, who would have chosen joy at once,
now while her hair sparked as she brushed it
    and her face was already sad with beauty's sadness
    and had no need for the marks of care—
      (yes, surely she did choose so:
          the tale as told breaks down, grows
                      vague)
—how she laughed when she found her Destiny
          tucked under seven quilts of down,
laughed at the ball of silk
held out impatiently by those fingers of bone,
all that power half asleep on the cloudy mountain!

Catherine threw down her cloak on Destiny's bed
for an eighth coverlid,
and merrily took the thread,
stepped out of her youth's brocade slippers
       and set out barefoot, strong from her years of
                         pleasure,
    to wander the roads of the second half of her life.

An Embroidery   (III) Red Snow

(*after one of the* Parables from
Nature *by Mrs. Gatty*)

Crippled with desire, he questioned it.
Evening upon the heights, juice of the pomegranate:
who could connect it with sunlight?

He took snow into his
red from cold hands.
It would not acknowledge the blood inside,
stayed white, melted only.

And all summer, beyond how many plunging valleys,
                              remote, verdant lesser peaks,
still there were fields
                by day silver,
                hidden often in thunderheads,
but faithful before night, crimson.
He knew it was red snow.

He grows tall, and sets out.
The story, inexorably, is of arrival long after, by dark.
Tells he stood waiting
                bewildered
                        in stinging silver towards dawn,
                        and looked over abysses, back:

        the height of his home, snowy, red,
        taunted him.   Fable snuffs out.
                                        What did he do?

                        He grew old.
                        With bloodbright hands he wrought
                icy monuments.
        Beard and long hair flying he rode the whirlwind,
keening the praises of red snow.

35

An Embroidery   (IV) Swiss Cheese

(after a lost poem, 1947)

Lost wooden poem,
cows and people wending
downmountain slowly
to wooden homesteads

cows first, the families
following calmly their swaying,
their pausing, their moving ahead in dreamy
constancy.
Children asleep in arms of old men,
healthy pallor of smooth cheeks facing
back to high pastures left for the day,
are borne down as the light
waits to leave.

Upper air glows with motes color of hay,
deep valley darkens.
Lost poem, I know
the cows were fragrant
and sounds were of hooves and feet on earth,
of clumps of good grass torn off, to chew
slowly; and not much talk.
They were returning
to wooden buckets, to lantern-beams
crisp as new straw.

Swiss cheese with black bread,
meadow, wood walls, what

did I do with you, I'm looking
through holes, in cheese, or
pine knotholes, and

who were those peaceful folk, the poem
was twenty years ago, I need it now.

WANTING THE MOON

The beating of the wings.
Unheard.
        The beat rising from dust
        of gray streets
        as now off pale fields.

'A huge crowd of
friends and well-wishers . . .'
                  Someone
figureskates brilliantly
across the lacquer lid of a box
where dreams are stored.
Something
        has to give.

The wings unheard
             felt as a rush of air,
        of air withdrawn, the breath
taken—
        The blow falls,
        feather and bone
                stone-heavy.
I am felled,
        rise up
        with changed vision,
      a singing in my ears.

Not the moon. A flower
on the other side of the water.

The water sweeps past in flood,
dragging a whole tree by the hair,

a barn, a bridge. The flower
sings on the far bank.

Not a flower, a bird calling,
hidden among the darkest trees, music

over the water, making a silence
out of the brown folds of the river's cloak.

The moon. No, a young man walking
under the trees.   There are lanterns

among the leaves.
Tender, wise, merry,

his face is awake with its own light,
I see it across the water as if close up.

A jester.   The music rings from his bells,
gravely, a tune of sorrow,

I dance to it on my riverbank.

Not to have but to be.
The black heart of the poppy,
O to lie there as seed.

To become the belovéd.
As the world ends, to enter
the last note of its music.

Wanting the Moon   **(II)**

Not the moon.   To be a bronze head
inhabited by a god.
       A torso of granite
left out in the weather ten thousand years,
adored by passing clouds.
Their shadows painting it, brushstrokes of dust blue.
Giving themselves to it in infinite rain.
    To be a cloud. Sated with wandering, seize
the gaiety of change from within, of dissolution,
of raining.
       To lie down in the dreams
of a young man whose hair
is the color of mahogany.

A Cloak

'For there's more enterprise
In walking naked.'
W. B. Yeats

And I walked naked
from the beginning

breathing in
my life,
breathing out
poems,

arrogant in innocence.

But of the song-clouds my breath made
in cold air

a cloak has grown,
white and,
            where here a word
            there another
froze, glittering,
stone-heavy.

A mask I had not meant
to wear, as if of frost,
covers my face.
            Eyes looking out,
a longing silent at song's core.

A Defeat

            Wanted
to give away pride,
like donating one oil well when you know
you own a whole delta.

Gave away nothing: no takers.
The derricks are idle.

Punt through the shallows,
pushing fat lilies aside,
my shadow,
            in your dark boat.

Craving

Wring the swan's neck, seeking
a little language of drops of blood.

How can we speak of blood, the sky
is drenched with it.

A little language
of dew, then.

It dries.

A language
of leaves underfoot.
Leaves on the tree, trembling
in speech. Poplars
            tremble and speak
if you draw near them.

43

Swan that sings and
                 does not die.
Aimless, the long neck stretched out,
the note held, death
withheld.   Wings
creaking in strong flight,
not,
     not giving way,
weary of strength

                 the music
ending without conclusion

Earth Dust

So slowly I am dying
you wouldn't know it.
They say birth begins it.
                    But for three decades, four,
             the sky's valves lie open,
                 or close to open over again,
a green pearl revealed.

Slowly, slowly,
I spin towards the sun.

44

I am waiting.
On benches, at the corners
of earth's waitingrooms,
by trees whose sap rises, rises
to escape in gray leaves and lose
itself in the last air.
Waiting
for who comes at last,
late, lost, the forever
longed-for, walking
not my road but crossing
the corner where I wait.

Someone imagined
who was real too

and did not want me to
imagine him,
to violate

his dream of himself.

. . . .

The touch of dream
upon the fine white

skin of someone caught
in someone else's imagined life.

Nails of imagination
tenderly scratching the back of

someone who isn't there,
who's there heavy-hearted,

and won't look up.

. . . .

Who won't look up to enter
the dream that violates
his imagined order.

Gently, insistently,
re-entering
the order of himself,

inviolate dream,
unimagined.

Mad Song

My madness is dear to me.
I who was almost always the sanest among my friends,
one to whom others came for comfort,
now at my breasts (that look timid and ignorant,
        that don't look as if milk had flowed from them,
        years gone by)
cherish a viper.
          Hail, little serpent of useless longing
that may destroy me,
that bites me with such idle
needle teeth.

I who am loved by those who love me
for honesty,
to whom life was an honest breath
          taken in good faith,
I've forgotten how to tell joy from bitterness.

Dear to me, dear to me,
blue poison, green pain in the mind's veins.
How am I to be cured against my will?

The Gulf   (II)

(Late December, 1968)

'My soul's a black boy with a long way to go.
a long way to know if black is beautiful.'
'But doesn't your soul fly, don't you know who you are?'

'Flies, has flown, yes, poems and praise
known to it—but like a worn kite, old silk
mended with paper,

                    bucks the wind, falters, leans
sideways, is falling.'
                    'And you spoke of it
as a boy?'
          'That boy with long, cold
stems of stolen gladioli aching his arms:
No place to go.'

A Hunger

Black beans, white sunlight.
These have sufficed.

Approval of mothers, of brothers,
of strangers—a plunge of the hands
in sifted flour, over the wrists.
It gives pleasure.

And being needed. Being loved for that.
Being forgiven.

What mountains there are
to border solitude and provide
limits, blue or
dark as raisins.

But hunger: a hunger there is
refuses. Refuses the earth.

A stealth in air that means:

the swallows have flown
south while I flew
north again.

Still, in the quiet there are
chickadees,
to make me grudgingly smile,
and crickets curious about
my laundry put out to bleach
on brown grass.

So I do smile.
What else to do?
Melancholy is boring.

And if the well goes dry—
and it has;
and if the body-count goes up—
and it does;
and if the summer spent
itself before I took it
into my life—?

Nothing to do but take
crumbs that fall from the chickadee's table
—or starve.
But the time for starving is not yet.

Up the long street of castles, over cobbles
we rode at twilight, alone.

Harlech, Duino, Azay-le-Rideau,
and many more,

neighboring one another.
Of all the windows

none were lit. The sky shone
in some, pale.

Through silence moved
the creak of saddles, jingle of gear.
Uphill,

though not very steep,
the road lay, and was white.

High stepped the horses' feet.

But as I woke I saw I could not see
who that belovéd was that rode with me.

No reason: hyacinthine, ordinary,
extraordinary, creature:

on your two legs, running,
the grey brain above
transmitting its poetry—

just that you are, man, someone,
wings at your heels, the gods sent

to tell me.

Adam's Complaint

Some people,
no matter what you give them,
still want the moon.

The bread,
the salt,
white meat and dark,
still hungry.

The marriage bed
and the cradle,
still empty arms.

You give them land,
their own earth under their feet,
still they take to the roads.

And water: dig them the deepest well,
still it's not deep enough
to drink the moon from.

Trying to remember old dreams. A voice. Who came in.
And meanwhile the rain, all day, all evening,
quiet steady sound. Before it grew too dark
I watched the blue iris leaning under the rain,
the flame of the poppies guttered and went out.
A voice. Almost recalled. There have been times
the gods entered. Entered a room, a cave?
A long enclosure where I was, the fourth wall of it
too distant or too dark to see. The birds are silent,
no moths at the lit windows. Only a swaying rosebush
pierces the table's reflection, raindrops gazing from it.
There have been hands laid on my shoulders.
                    What has been said to me,
            how has my life replied?
The rain, the rain . . .

Two fading red spots mark on my thighs
where a flea from the fur of a black, curly, yearning dog
bit me, casually, and returned into the fur.

Melanie was the dog's name. That afternoon
she had torn the screen from a door and littered fragments
of screen everywhere, and of chewed-up paper,

stars, whole constellations of paper, glimmered
in shadowy floor corners. She had been punished, adequately;
this was not a first offense. And forgiven,

but sadly: her master knew she would soon discover
other ways to show forth her discontent, her black humor.
Meanwhile, standing on hind legs like a human child,

she came to lean her body, her arms and head,
in my lap. I was a friendly stranger. She gave me
a share of her loneliness, her warmth, her flea.

Between chores—
                    hulling strawberries,
                    answering letters—
or between poems,

returning to the mirror
to see if I'm there.

Plié, the knees bend,
a frog flexing to spring;
grand battement, the taut leg
flails as if to beat
chaff from the wheat;
attitude, Hermes brings
ambiguous messages
and moves dream-smoothly
yet with hidden strain
that breaks in sweat,
into *arabesque* that traces
swan-lines on vision's stone
that the dancer not seeing
herself, feels in the bone.
Coupé, the air is cut
out from under the foot,
grand jeté, glissade, grand jeté, glissade,
the joy of leaping, of moving by
leaps and bounds, of gliding
to leap, and gliding
to leap becomes, while it lasts,
heart pounding, breath hurting,
the deepest, the only joy.

Where there is violet in the green of the sea
the eye rests, knowing
a depth there.
In the depth where the violet changes, the sea
surrenders to the eye
a knowledge.
Where the blue of shadow rests upon green the sea
knows desire, sorrow
becomes joy
where there is violet in the eye of the sea.
In the changing
depth of desire
the I knows it is open, the distant sea
withholds nothing, surrenders
nothing,
save to the eye. Rests in the sea
desire of joy,
heart's
sorrow. Where there is violet in the green of the sea.

Whó am I? Whó am I?
It is the old cry wandering in the wind
and with it interwoven
words of reply: I am fiery ember, dispersed
in innumerable fragments
flying in the wind, gray cinders
and black, and all still burning, all bearing
a point of flame
hidden in ashes. Flying upon the nameless
winds and upon those that men
know and name: sirocco,
bise, northeaster, tramontana. I die and again
life is breathed
into me. Whó am I? Whó am I?
My dust burns
in the past and flies before me
into the whirling future,
the Old World, the New World, my soul is scattered
across the continents
in the named places and the named and unnamed
shadowy faces, my years
a hearth from which the sparks wander
and to its stones
blow back at random upon the winds
to kindle the brand again that fades and flares.

Black,
  shining with a yellowish
  dew,
erect,
  revealed by the laughing
  glance of Krishna's eyes:
the terrible lotus.

Topmost leaves of young oak,
    young maple,
        are red—a delicate red
almost maroon.

I am not young,
    and not yet old. Young enough not to be able
        to imagine my own old age. Something in me

puts out new leaves that are red also,
    delicate, fantastic, in June,
        early summer, late spring in the north.

A dark time we live in. One would think
    there would be no summer. No red leaves.
        One would think there would be

no drawings-up of the blind at morning
    to a field awake with flowers.
        Yet with my tuft of new leaves

it is that field I wake to,
    a woman foolish with desire.

The Curve

Along the tracks
counting
always the right foot awarded
            the tie to step on
the left stumbling all the time in cinders

towards where
      an old caboose
samples of paint were once tried out on
is weathering in a saltmarsh
            to tints Giotto dreamed.

'Shall we
ever reach it?'   'Look—
the tracks take a curve.
We may
         come round to it
if we keep going.'

Somehow nineteen years ago
    clumsily passionate
I drew into me the seed
of a man—
        and bore it, cast it out—

man-seed that grew
        and became a person
        whose subtle mind and quick heart

    though I beat him, hurt him,
    while I fed him, loved him,

now stand beyond me, out in the world
        beyond my skin
beautiful and strange as if
    I had given birth to a tree.

A Marigold from North Vietnam

for Barbara Deming

Marigold   resurrection flower
that the dead   love and come forth
by candlelight to inhale
scent of   sharp   a smoke-of-watchfires
odor.   The living
taste it as if   on the tongue
acrid.   In summer it tells   of fall
in fall   of winter   in winter
of spring.   The leaves
very fine   delicate.   The flowers
petal-crowded   long-lasting.
Drooping in dryness   the whole plant
in minutes   lifts itself   resilient
given water.   The earth in the pot was dug
in quick kindness   by moonlight   for gift
in Maine   but to the root-threads cling still
some crumbs of Vietnam.   When I water
the marigold these too   are moistened
and give forth   nourishment.

How easy it is to return
into the great nowhere!

Two weeks incommunicado
on the border of somebody else's life
equals two months at sea.

Whom did I anciently
pine for? What were my passions?

The plains of the sea
modulate quiet songs that light
hums to itself.
                    The decks
are holystoned. Smoothly
the ship makes way, no shoreline
to mark her passage.

The wake fading.
Translated.

If even so I tremble sometimes,
if I scan the horizon for land-shadow;

it is because I am so unused
to the sufficiency of
random essentials:

moon, box, marigold, *Two Hundred and One
French Verbs.*

I practise breathing, my spirit acquires
color and texture of unbleached linen.

I am unused to
the single ocean,
the one moon.

Secret Festival; September Moon

Pandemonium of owls
plying from east to west and
west to east, over the full-moon sea of
mown grass.
                    The low-voiced
and the wailing high-voiced
hooting together, neither in dialogue
                    nor in unison,
                                   an overlapping
antiphonal a fox
                 barks to,
as if to excel, whose obligato
the owls ignore.
They raise
the roof of the dark; ferocious
          their joy in the extreme silver
                    the moon has floated out from itself,
luminous air in which their eyes
don't hurt or close,
                    the night of the year
               their incantations have raised—
               and if
foxes believe it's theirs, there's enough to slip
over and round them, earthlings, of owlish fire.

The moon tiger.
In the room, here.
It came in, it is
prowling sleekly
under and over
the twin beds.
See its small head,
silver smooth,
hear the pad of its
large feet. Look,
its white stripes
in the light that slid
through the jalousies.
It is sniffing our
clothes, its cold nose
nudges our bodies.
The beds are narrow,
but I'm coming in with you.

Crackle and flash almost in the kitchen sink—the
thunderclap follows even as I
jump back frightened,
afraid to touch metal—

        The roofgutters pouring down
          whole rivers, making holes in the earth—
  The electric bulbs fade and go out,
     another thin crackling lights the window
and in the instant before the next onslaught of kettle-
                         drums,

a small bird, I don't know its name,
among the seagreen tossed leaves
               begins its song.

'That creep Tolstoy,' she sobbed.
'He. . . He. . . couldn't even. . .'
Something about his brother dying.

The serfs' punishments
have not ceased to suppurate on their backs.
Woodlots. People. Someone crying

under the yellow
autumn birchgrove drove him
wild: A new set of resolves:

When gambling, that almost obsolete fever,
or three days with the gypsies
sparked him into pure ego, he could,

just the same, write home, 'Sell them.'
It's true. 'Still,' (someone who loved her said,
cold and firm while she dissolved,

hypocrite, in self disgust, *lectrice*)
'Still, he kept on. He wrote
all that he wrote; and seems to have understood

better than most of us:
to be human isn't easy. It's not
easy to be a serf or a master and learn

that art. It takes nerve. Bastard. Fink.
Yet the grief
trudging behind his funeral, he earned.'

My sign!
      —yours, too—
anyone's—
          aloft in the coppery
afterglow, gulls or pigeons,
         too high to tell,
way above downtown highrise
wheeling serene,
             whether to feed or
for flight's sake
         makes no difference
sliding the air's
         mountains,
unhastening

the bows of their winged bodies drawn
sostenuto over the hover of
        smoke, grey gauze tinged with rust:
over the traffic of our lives—a sign
if I look up—
        or you—
anyone.

i

At the dump bullfrogs
converse as usual.
It's their swamp
        below the garbage tip,
where they were masters
long before towns had
dumps.   Rapid
the crossfire of their
utterance.
Their eyes
                are at water level.
Rats prowl
among the soiled bulrushes.
The frogs sound angry.
        But they have not
        hopped away in the time of rains.
        They inhabit their heritage,
        pluck the twilight
                        pleasurably.
Are they irascible?
Yes, but not bored.
        It is summer,
        their spirits are high.
Urgently,
        anxiously,
above their glistening heads,
                        fireflies
            switch
            on and
                        off.

ii

The fireflies desperately
entreat their unknown bridegrooms,
their somewhere brides,
            to discover them.
                    Now while there is time.
But what of the moths?
Their lives also are brief,
but hour after hour—
                    their days and years—
they choose to cling upon windows
ingazing to lighted rooms.
Silk of their bodies unruffled,
dust on spread wings unsmirched.

            Their eyes' lamps
            when mens' lights are put out
            glow steadily—they try
            still to look in towards departed splendor
that may return?

            What secret, worth
            this impassioned stillness
is it they dream of?

I want some funny jazz band
      to wake me,
tell me life's been dreaming me.
I want something like love, but made
      all of string or pebbles,
      oboe of torn air
to tear me to my senses.
        Emily's black birds
don't bate their banjos nor the throbbing
      of their quick hearts.
The leaves part to reveal
      more leaves, and darkness,
      darkness and the intense
      poised sequence of leaves.
I want to take the last of all leaves
        between my lips and taste
          its weight of stone.

Burden, grace,
artifice coiled
brittle on my back, integral,

I thought to crawl
out of you,

yearned for the worm's
lowly freedom that can go

under earth and whose
slow arrow pierces
the thick of dark

but in my shell
my life was,

and when I knew it
I remembered

my eyes adept to witness
air and harsh light

and look all ways.

A TREE TELLING OF ORPHEUS

A Tree Telling of Orpheus

White dawn. Stillness.   When the rippling began
    I took it for sea-wind, coming to our valley with rumors
    of salt, of treeless horizons. But the white fog
didn't stir; the leaves of my brothers remained outstretched,
unmoving.
        Yet the rippling drew nearer—and then
my own outermost branches began to tingle, almost as if
fire had been lit below them, too close, and their twig-tips
were drying and curling.
                Yet I was not afraid, only
                deeply alert.

I was the first to see him, for I grew
        out on the pasture slope, beyond the forest.
He was a man, it seemed: the two
moving stems, the short trunk, the two
arm-branches, flexible, each with five leafless
                    twigs at their ends,
and the head that's crowned by brown or gold grass,
bearing a face not like the beaked face of a bird,
    more like a flower's.
                He carried a burden made of
some cut branch bent while it was green,
strands of a vine tight-stretched across it. From this,
when he touched it, and from his voice
which unlike the wind's voice had no need of our
leaves and branches to complete its sound,
                    came the ripple.
But it was now no longer a ripple (he had come near and
stopped in my first shadow) it was a wave that bathed me
      as if rain
              rose from below and around me
        instead of falling.
And what I felt was no longer a dry tingling:

I seemed to be singing as he sang, I seemed to know
what the lark knows; all my sap
          was mounting towards the sun that by now
                    had risen, the mist was rising, the grass
was drying, yet my roots felt music moisten them
deep under earth.

                    He came still closer, leaned on my trunk:
                    the bark thrilled like a leaf still-folded.
Music! There was no twig of me not
                              trembling with joy and fear.

Then as he sang
it was no longer sounds only that made the music:
he spoke, and as no tree listens I listened, and language
                    came into my roots
                              out of the earth,
                    into my bark
                              out of the air,
                    into the pores of my greenest shoots
                              gently as dew
and there was no word he sang but I knew its meaning.
He told of journeys,
              of where sun and moon go while we stand in dark,
     of an earth-journey he dreamed he would take some day
deeper than roots . . .
He told of the dreams of man, wars, passions, griefs,
          and I, a tree, understood words—ah, it seemed
my thick bark would split like a sapling's that
                              grew too fast in the spring
when a late frost wounds it.

                              Fire he sang,
that trees fear, and I, a tree, rejoiced in its flames.
New buds broke forth from me though it was full summer.
          As though his lyre (now I knew its name)
          were both frost and fire, its chords flamed
up to the crown of me.

I was seed again.
                    I was fern in the swamp.
                         I was coal.

And at the heart of my wood
(so close I was to becoming man or a god)
          there was a kind of silence, a kind of sickness,
               something akin to what men call boredom,
                                             something
(the poem descended a scale, a stream over stones)
                    that gives to a candle a coldness
                         in the midst of its burning, he said.

It was then,
               when in the blaze of his power that
                              reached me and changed me
          I thought I should fall my length,
that the singer began
                    to leave me.   Slowly
               moved from my noon shadow
                                        to open light,
words leaping and dancing over his shoulders
back to me
               rivery sweep of lyre-tones becoming
slowly again
               ripple.

And I
          in terror
               but not in doubt of
                              what I must do
in anguish, in haste,
                    wrenched from the earth root after root,
the soil heaving and cracking, the moss tearing asunder—
and behind me the others: my brothers
forgotten since dawn. In the forest
they too had heard,

and were pulling their roots in pain
out of a thousand years' layers of dead leaves,
            rolling the rocks away,
                        breaking themselves
                                    out of
                                    their depths.
You would have thought we would lose the sound of the lyre,
                        of the singing
so dreadful the storm-sounds were, where there was no storm,
                no wind but the rush of our
            branches moving, our trunks breasting the air.
            But the music!
                        The music reached us.

Clumsily,
            stumbling over our own roots,
                        rustling our leaves
                                    in answer,
we moved, we followed.

All day we followed, up hill and down.
                                    We learned to dance,
for he would stop, where the ground was flat,
                                    and words he said
taught us to leap and to wind in and out
around one another   in figures   the lyre's measure designed.
The singer
            laughed till he wept to see us, he was so glad.
                                    At sunset
we came to this place I stand in, this knoll
with its ancient grove that was bare grass then.
            In the last light of that day his song became
farewell.
            He stilled our longing.
            He sang our sun-dried roots back into earth,
watered them: all-night rain of music so quiet

we could almost

not hear it in the

moonless dark.

By dawn he was gone.

We have stood here since,

in our new life.

We have waited.

He does not return.

It is said he made his earth-journey, and lost
what he sought.

It is said they felled him
and cut up his limbs for firewood.

And it is said

his head still sang and was swept out to sea singing.

Perhaps he will not return.

But what we have lived

comes back to us.

We see more.

We feel, as our rings increase,

something that lifts our branches, that stretches our furthest

leaf-tips

further.

The wind, the birds,

do not sound poorer but clearer,

recalling our agony, and the way we danced.

The music!

RELEARNING THE ALPHABET

I want to give away the warm coat
I bought but found
cold and ungainly.
                    A man's wife will wear it,
            and in exchange the man will tear
an ugly porch off an old empty house,

leave it the way it was,
bare and sightly.

'I am an object to you,' he said.
'My charm, what you call
my charm—
            alien to me.'
'No! No!' she is crying.
'Indissoluble—'The tears hurt her throat.
'—idiosyncratic—you—not an object—'

                        (That smiling glance from under
                        fair-lashed long lids—complicit—
                        :he cannot help it.)

            'Fire of the mind—
your vision—unique—
aware the lynx is there in smoky light,
a god disdained, unrecognized, dragged in darkness
out to sea—'

Fire, light, again,
beginning to dry tears: awaken, illumine.
Pain tears at her with lynx claws
but her throat relaxes.
Still he suspects. (—Not I but your idea
                of who I am.)
                        (Why should he care,
                        not wanting the love I keep holding out
                        stupidly, like a warm coat on a hot day?)

She reflects out loud, 'Aren't all, whom we love,
not *objects*, but—symbols—impersonal—
molten glass in our desire, their dailiness
translucent—?
                The gods in us,
you said: what violence more brutish
than not to see them:

              I am not doing you
              that violence:
                                    I see
what is strange in you, and surpasses
with its presence your history . . .'

But she knows the wall is there she can't pass.
The god, the light, the fire,
live in his body she may not touch.
It does not want to touch hers.
Tropism, one of those words she always
had to look up, before its meaning
took root in her, says itself back of her tongue.
She is dark,
            a blackness sinks on her.—*He has*
no tropism towards me, that knowledge.
And yet, and yet, he wants to be known to her,
hungers for love—even from *her* dark source—
      not to pass godlike from form to form, but dig in its
                                                        claws:
even now, love that he does not want.

And he—(he does not say it now, there's nothing
              said now but re-sayings, but it was written already,
              she has the letter)
'You know
better than I
the desolation is gestation. Absence
                        an absolute
                        presence
                        calling forth
                        the person   (the poet)
                  into desperate continuance, toward
                  fragments of light.'

                              89

Relearning the Alphabet

(June, 1968—April, 1969)

For G. who could not help it, I. who saw me,
R. who read me, and M. for everything.

"The treasure . . . lies buried. There is no need
to seek it in a distant country . . . It is behind
the stove, the center of the life and warmth
that rule our existence, if only we knew how to
unearth it. And yet—there is this strange and
persistent fact, that it is only after . . . a jour-
ney in a distant region, in a new land, that . . .
the inner voice . . . can make itself understood
by us. And to this strange and persistent fact is
added another: that he who reveals to us the
meaning of our . . . inward pilgrimage must be
himself a stranger . . ."

—Heinrich Zimmer

A

Joy—a beginning.   Anguish, ardor.
To relearn the ah! of knowing in unthinking
joy: the belovéd stranger lives.
Sweep up anguish as with a wing-tip,
brushing the ashes back to the fire's core.

B

To be. To love an other only for being.

C

Clear, cool? Not those evasions. The seeing
that burns through, comes through to
the fire's core.

D

In the beginning was delight. A depth
stirred as one stirs fire unthinking.
Dark   dark   dark   . And the blaze illumines
dream.

E

Endless
returning, endless
revolution of dream to ember, ember to anguish,
anguish to flame, flame to delight,
delight to dark and dream, dream to ember

F

that the mind's fire may not fail.
The *vowels of affliction,* of unhealed
not to feel it, uttered,
transformed in utterance
to song.
            Not farewell, not farewell, but faring

G

forth into the grace of transformed
continuance, the green meadows
of Grief-Dale where joy grew, flowering
close to the ground, old tales recount,

H

and may be had yet for the harvesting.

.

I, J

Into the world of continuance, to find
I-who-I-am again, who wanted
to enter a life not mine,
        to leap a wide, deep, swift river.

At the edge, I stand yet. No, I am moving away,
walking away from the unbridged rush of waters towards
'Imagination's holy forest,' meaning to thread its ways,
        that are dark,
and come to my own clearing, where 'dreamy, gloomy,
friendly trees' grow, one by one—but
        I'm not looking where I'm going,
        my head's turned back, to see
        whom I called 'jester': someone dreamed
        on the far bank: not dreamed, seen
in epiphany, as Picasso's bronze *Head of a Jester*
was seen.
        I go stumbling
            (head turned)
                back to my origins:
(if that's where I'm going)
        to joy, my Jerusalem.

Weeping, gesturing,
I'm a small figure in mind's eye,
diminishing in the sweep of rain or gray tears
that cloud the far shore as jealous rage
clouds love and changes it, changes vision.

.

K

Caritas is what I must travel to.
Through to the fire's core,
an alchemy:
                    caritas, claritas.
But find my face clenched
when I wake at night
                    in limbo.

L

Back there forgetting, among the
letters   folded and put away.
Not uttered.
                    'The feel of
not to feel it
was never said . . .' Keats said.
'Desolation . . . Absence an absolute
presence
            calling forth . . .' the jester said
from the far shore ('gravely, ringing his bells,
a tune of sorrow.' I dance to it?)
'You are offhand. The trouble
is concealed?' Isak said,
calling me forth.

.

93

I am called forth
from time to time.

I was in the time
of desolation.
What light is it
waking me?
            Absence has not become
a presence.
                Lost in the alphabet
                I was looking for
                the word I can't now say
(love)
            and am called forth
            unto the twelfth letter
            by the love in a question.

                        •

M

Honest man, I wanted
                the moon and went
                out to sea to touch
                the moon and

                down a lane of bright
                broken vanishing
                curled pyramids of
                moonwater
                moving
                towards the moon
            and touched
            the luminous dissolving
            half moon
            cold

94

I am
come back,
humbled, to warm myself,
honest man,

our bed is
          upon the earth
your soul is
          in your body
your mouth
          has found
my mouth once more
—I'm home.

N

Something in me that wants to cling
to *never*,
          wants to have been
          wounded deeper
          burned by the cold moon to cinder,

shrinks as the disk
dwindles to vision
                    numb not to continuance
                    but to that source
                    of mind's fire

                    waning now,
                    no doubt to wax again—

                    yet I perhaps not be there
                    in its light.

O

Hostile.   Ordinary.   Home.
Order.   Alone.   Other.

Hostile longing.   Ordinary rose, omnivorous.
                Home, solitude.

Somnolence grotto.
Caught. Lost. Orient almost,
volition.
Own.   Only.

Pain recedes, rising from heart to head
and out.

                Apple thunder, rolling over the
attic floor.

                        Yet I would swear
                        there had been savage light
                        moments before.

P, Q

In childhood dream-play I was always
the knight or squire, not
the lady:
quester, petitioner, win or lose, not
she who was sought.
The initial of quest or question
branded itself long since on the flank
of my Pegasus.
Yet he flies always
home to the present.

R

Released through bars of sorrow
as if not a gate had opened but I
grown intangible had passed through, shadowy,
from dark of yearning into
a soft day, western March;

a thrust of birdsong
parts the gold flowers thickbranching
that roof the path over.

Arms enfold me
tenderly. I am trusted, I trust
the real that transforms me.
                    And relinquish
                    in grief
the seeing that burns through, comes through
to fire's core: transformation, continuance,
                    as acts of magic I would perform, are no longer
                    articles of faith.

                    ·

S

Or no: it
slowly becomes known to me:
articles of faith are indeed
rules of the will—graceless,
                    faithless.
The door I flung my weight against
was constructed to open   out
                              towards me.
In-seeing
to candleflame's
blue ice-cavern, measureless,

may not be forced by sharp
desire.
          The Prince
          turns in the wood: 'Retrace
                              thy steps, seek out
          the hut you passed, impatient,
          the day you lost your quarry.

There dwells
a secret. Restore to it
its life.
You will not recognize
your desire until
thou hast it fast, it goeth
aside, it hath
the cunning of quicksilver.'

.

I turn in the forest.
About me the tree-multitudes
twist their roots in earth
to rip it, draw
hidden rivers up into
branch-towers.
Their crowns in the light sway
green beyond vision.
                      All utterance
takes me step by hesitant step towards

T

—yes, to continuance: into
                                that life beyond the dead-end where
(in a desert time of
dry strange heat, of dust
that tinged mountain clouds with copper,
turn of the year impending unnoticed,
the cactus shadows brittle thornstars,
time of
desolation)   I was lost.

.

98

The forest is holy.
The sacred paths are of stone.
A clearing.
The altars are shifting deposits of pineneedles,
            hidden waters,
            streets of choirwood,
not what the will
thinks to construct for its testimonies.

U

Relearn the alphabet,
relearn the world, the world
understood anew only in doing, under-
stood only as
looked-up-into out of earth,
the heart an eye looking,
the heart a root
planted in earth.
Transmutation is not
under the will's rule.

V

Vision sets out
journeying somewhere,
walking the dreamwaters:
arrives
not on the far shore but upriver,
a place not evoked, discovered.

                        •

W

Heart breaks but mends
like good bone.

It's the vain will
wants to have been wounded deeper,
burned by the cold moon to cinder.

Wisdom's a stone
dwells in forgotten pockets—
lost, refound, exiled—
revealed again
in the palm of
mind's hand, moonstone
of wax and wane, stone pulse.

Y

Vision will not be used.
Yearning will not be used.
Wisdom will not be used.
Only the vain will
strives to use and be used,
comes not to fire's core
but cinder.

Z

Sweep up
anguish as with a wing-tip:

the blaze addresses
a different darkness:
absence has not become
the transformed presence the will
looked for,
but other: the present,

that which was poised already in the ah! of praise.

Silent, about-to-be-parted-from house.
Wood creaking, trying to sigh, impatient.
Clicking of squirrel-teeth in the attic.
Denuded beds, couches stripped of serapes.

Deep snow shall block all entrances
and oppress the roof and darken
the windows.   O Lares,
don't leave.
The house yawns like a bear.
Guard its profound dreams for us,
that it return to us when we return.

TO STAY ALIVE (1971)

As one goes on living and working, themes recur, transposed into another key perhaps. Single poems that seemed isolated perceptions when one wrote them prove to have struck the first note of a scale or a melody. I have heard professors of literature snicker with embarrassment because a poet quoted himself: they thought it immodest, narcissistic. Their attitude, a common one, reveals a failure to understand that though *the artist as craftsman* is engaged in making discrete and autonomous works—each of which, like a chair or a table, will have, as Ezra Pound said, the requisite number of legs and not wobble—yet at the same time, more unconsciously, as these attempts accumulate over the years, *the artist as explorer in language of the experiences of his or her life* is, willy-nilly, weaving a fabric, building a whole in which each discrete work is a part that functions in some way in relation to all the others. It happens at times that the poet becomes aware of the relationships that exist between poem and poem; is conscious, after the act, of one poem, one line or stanza, having been the precursor of another. It may be years later; and then, to get the design clear—'for himself and *thereby* for others,' Ibsen put it—he must in honesty pick up that thread, bring the cross reference into its rightful place in the inscape, the Gestalt of his life (his work)/his work (his life).

In *Relearning the Alphabet* I published some sections of a poem then called, as a working title, 'From a Notebook,' which I was aware was 'unfinished,' open-ended. In pursuing it further I came to realize that the long poem 'An Interim,' published in a different section of the same volume, was really a prelude or introduction to the Notebook poem. And Mitch Goodman and Hayden Carruth, on reading new parts of the Notebook, showed me that other, earlier poems—such as those I had written about my sister Olga after her death in 1964, and included in *The Sorrow Dance* —had a relation to it that seemed to demand their reissue in

105

juxtaposition. It was Hayden who, years ago, pointed out to me how, in writing about my childhood in England, my diction became English—and this fact becomes itself one of the themes of the Notebook poem; for the sense my individual history gives me of being straddled between *places* extends to the more universal sense any writer my age—rooted in a cultural past barely shared by younger readers, yet committed to a solidarity of hope and struggle with the revolutionary young—must have of being almost unbearably, painfully, straddled across *time*.

In the pendant to 'Olga Poems'—A Note to Olga (1966) two years after her death—occurs the first mention in my work of one of those public occasions, demonstrations, that have become for many of us such familiar parts of our lives. Later, not as a deliberate repetition but because the events were of importance to me, other such occasions were spoken of in other poems. The sense of community, of fellowship, experienced in the People's Park in Berkeley in 1969, deepened and intensified under the vicious police attack that, for middle-class whites especially, was so instructive. The personal response that moves from the identification of my lost sister, as a worker for human rights, with the pacifists 'going limp' as they are dragged to the paddywagon in Times Square in 1966, to the understanding by 1970 that 'there comes a time when only anger/is love,' is one shared by many of us who have come bit by bit to the knowledge that opposition to war, whose foul air we have breathed so long that by now we are almost choked forever by it, cannot be separated from opposition to the whole system of insane greed, of racism and imperialism, of which war is only the inevitable expression. In 'Prologue: An Interim' some of my heroes—that is, those who stand for integrity, honesty, love of life—are draft resisters who go to jail in testimony of their refusal to take part in carnage. In the same poem I invoked the self-immolators—Vietnamese and American—not as models but as flares to keep us moving in the dark. I spoke with love—a love I still feel—of those who 'disdain to kill.' But later I found that Gandhi himself had said it was better to 'cultivate the art of killing and being killed rather than in a cowardly manner to flee from danger.' In the later sections of the Notebook the sense of who the guardians of life, of integrity, are, is extended to include not only those who 'disdain to kill' but all who struggle, violently if need be, to pull down this obscene system before it destroys all life on earth.

The justification, then, of including in a new volume poems which are available in other collections, is esthetic—it assembles separated parts of a whole. And I am given courage to do so by the hope of that whole being seen as having some value not as mere 'confesssional' autobiography, but as a document of some historical value, a record of one person's inner/outer experience in America during the '60's and the beginning of the '70's, an experience which is shared by so many and transcends the peculiar details of each life, though it can only be expressed in and through such details.

DENISE LEVERTOV

PRELUDES

Olga Poems

(*Olga Levertoff, 1914–1964*)

i

By the gas-fire, kneeling
to undress,
scorching luxuriously, raking
her nails over olive sides, the red
waistband ring—

(And the little sister
beady-eyed in the bed—
or drowsy, was I? My head
a camera—)

Sixteen. Her breasts
round, round, and
dark-nippled—

who now these two months long
is bones and tatters of flesh in earth.

ii

The high pitch of
nagging insistence, lines
creased into raised brows—

Ridden, ridden—
the skin around the nails
nibbled sore—

You wanted
to shout the world to its senses,
did you?—to browbeat

the poor into joy's
socialist republic—
What rage

and human shame swept you
when you were nine and saw
the Ley Street houses,

grasping their meaning as *slum*.
Where I, reaching that age,
teased you, admiring

architectural probity, circa
eighteen-fifty, and noted
pride in the whitened doorsteps.

Black one, black one,
there was a white
candle in your heart.

iii

i

Everything flows
            she muttered into my childhood,
pacing the trampled grass where human puppets
rehearsed fates that summer,
stung into alien semblances by the lash of her will—

112

everything flows—
I looked up from my Littlest Bear's cane armchair
and knew the words came from a book
and felt them alien to me

but linked to words we loved
                              from the hymnbook—*Time
like an ever-rolling stream / bears all its sons away—*

                    ii

Now as if smoke or sweetness were blown my way
I inhale a sense of her livingness in that instant,
feeling, dreaming, hoping, knowing boredom and zest like anyone
                                                          else—
a young girl in the garden, the same alchemical square
I grew in, we thought sometimes
too small for our grand destinies—
                              But dread
was in her, a bloodbeat, it was against the rolling dark
oncoming river she raised bulwarks, setting herself
to sift cinders after early Mass all of one winter,

labelling her desk's normal disorder, basing
her verses on Keble's *Christian Year,* picking
those endless arguments, pressing on

to manipulate lives to disaster . . . To change,
to change the course of the river! What rage for order
disordered her pilgrimage—so that for years at a time

she would hide among strangers, waiting
to rearrange all mysteries in a new light.

iii

Black one, incubus—
        she appeared
riding anguish as Tartars ride mares

over the stubble of bad years.

In one of the years
    when I didn't know if she were dead or alive
I saw her in dream

haggard and rouged
            lit by the flare
from an eel- or cockle-stand on a slum street—

was it a dream? I had lost

all sense, almost, of
    who she was, what—inside of her skin,
under her black hair
                dyed blonde—

it might feel like to be, in the wax and wane of the moon,
in the life I feel as unfolding, not flowing, the pilgrim years—

iv

On your hospital bed you lay
in love, the hatreds
that had followed you, a
comet's tail, burned out

as your disasters bred of love
burned out,
while pain and drugs
quarreled like sisters in you—

lay afloat on a sea
of love and pain—how you always
loved that cadence, 'Underneath
are the everlasting arms'—

all history
burned out, down
to the sick bone, save for

that kind candle.

v

i

In a garden grene whenas I lay—

you set the words to a tune so plaintive
it plucks its way through my life as through a wood.

As through a wood, shadow and light between birches,
gliding a moment in open glades, hidden by thickets of holly

your life winds in me.   In Valentines
a root protrudes from the greensward several yards from its tree

we might raise like a trapdoor's handle, you said,
and descend long steps to another country

where we would live without father or mother
and without longing for the upper world. *The birds
sang sweet,* O song, *in the midst of the daye,*

and we entered silent mid-Essex churches on hot afternoons
and communed with the effigies of knights and their ladies

and their slender dogs asleep at their feet,
the stone so cold—   *In youth*

is pleasure, in youth is pleasure.

ii

Under autumn clouds, under white
wideness of winter skies you went walking
the year you were most alone

returning to the old roads, seeing again
the signposts pointing to Theydon Garnon
or Stapleford Abbots or Greensted,

crossing the ploughlands (whose color I named *murple,*
a shade between brown and mauve that we loved
when I was a child and you

not much more than a child) finding new lanes
near White Roding or Abbess Roding; or lost in Romford's
new streets where there were footpaths then—

frowning as you ground out your thoughts, breathing deep
of the damp still air, taking
the frost into your mind unflinching.

How cold it was in your thin coat, your down-at-heel shoes—
tearless Niobe, your children were lost to you
and the stage lights had gone out, even the empty theater

was locked to you, cavern of transformation where all
had almost been possible.
                              How many books
you read in your silent lodgings that winter,
how the plovers transpierced your solitude out of doors with their
                                                    strange cries
I had flung open my arms to in longing, once, by your side
stumbling over the furrows—

Oh, in your torn stockings, with unwaved hair,
you were trudging after your anguish
over the bare fields, soberly, soberly.

vi

Your eyes were the brown gold of pebbles under water.
I never crossed the bridge over the Roding, dividing
the open field of the present from the mysteries,
the wraiths and shifts of time-sense Wanstead Park held suspended,
without remembering your eyes. Even when we were estranged
and my own eyes smarted in pain and anger at the thought of you.
And by other streams in other countries; anywhere where the light
reaches down through shallows to gold gravel. Olga's
brown eyes. One rainy summer, down in the New Forest,
when we could hardly breathe for ennui and the low sky,
you turned savagely to the piano and sightread
straight through all the Beethoven sonatas, day after day—
weeks, it seemed to me. I would turn the pages some of the time,
go out to ride my bike, return—you were enduring in the

falls and rapids of the music, the arpeggios rang out, the rectory
trembled, our parents seemed effaced.
I think of your eyes in that photo, six years before I was born,
the fear in them. What did you do with your fear,
later? Through the years of humiliation,
of paranoia and blackmail and near-starvation, losing
the love of those you loved, one after another,
parents, lovers, children, idolized friends, what kept
compassion's candle alight in you, that lit you
clear into another chapter (but the same book) 'a clearing
in the selva oscura,
a house whose door
swings open, a hand beckons
in welcome'?
                    I cross
so many brooks in the world, there is so much light
dancing on so many stones, so many questions my eyes
smart to ask of your eyes, gold brown eyes,
the lashes short but the lids
arched as if carved out of olivewood, eyes with some vision
of festive goodness in back of their hard, or veiled, or shining,
unknowable gaze. . .

May–August, 1964

118

A Note to Olga (1966)

i

Of lead and emerald
the reliquary
that knocks my breastbone,

slung round my neck
on a rough invisible rope
that rubs the knob of my spine.

Though I forget you
a red coal from your fire
burns in that box.

ii

On the Times Square sidewalk
we shuffle along, cardboard signs
—Stop the War—
slung round our necks.

The cops
hurry about,
shoulder to shoulder,
comic.

Your high soprano
sings out from just
in back of me—

We shall—I turn,
you're, I very well know,
not there,

and your voice, they say,
grew hoarse
from shouting at crowds. . .

yet *overcome*
sounds then hoarsely
from somewhere in front,

the paddywagon
gapes. —It seems
you that is lifted

limp and ardent
off the dark snow
and shoved in, and driven away.

The disasters numb within us
caught in the chest, rolling
in the brain like pebbles. The feeling
resembles lumps of raw dough

weighing down a child's stomach on baking day.
Or Rilke said it, 'My heart. . .
Could I say of it, it overflows
with bitterness . . . but no, as though

its contents were simply balled into
formless lumps, thus
do I carry it about.'
The same war

continues.
We have breathed the grits of it in, all our lives,
our lungs are pocked with it,
the mucous membrane of our dreams
coated with it, the imagination
filmed over with the gray filth of it:

the knowledge that humankind,

delicate Man, whose flesh
responds to a caress, whose eyes
are flowers that perceive the stars,

whose music excels the music of birds,
whose laughter matches the laughter of dogs,
whose understanding manifests designs
fairer than the spider's most intricate web,

still turns without surprise, with mere regret
to the scheduled breaking open of breasts whose milk
runs out over the entrails of still-alive babies,
transformation of witnessing eyes to pulp-fragments,
implosion of skinned penises into carcass-gulleys.

We are the humans, men who can make;
whose language imagines *mercy,*
lovingkindness; we have believed one another
mirrored forms of a God we felt as good—

who do these acts, who convince ourselves
it is necessary; these acts are done
to our own flesh; burned human flesh
is smelling in Vietnam as I write.

Yes, this is the knowledge that jostles for space
in our bodies along with all we
go on knowing of joy, of love;

our nerve filaments twitch with its presence
day and night,
nothing we say has not the husky phlegm of it in the saying,
nothing we do has the quickness, the sureness,
the deep intelligence living at peace would have.

What Were They Like?

1) Did the people of Vietnam
   use lanterns of stone?
2) Did they hold ceremonies
   to reverence the opening of buds?
3) Were they inclined to quiet laughter?
4) Did they use bone and ivory,
   jade and silver, for ornament?
5) Had they an epic poem?
6) Did they distinguish between speech and singing?

1) Sir, their light hearts turned to stone.
   It is not remembered whether in gardens
   stone lanterns illumined pleasant ways.
2) Perhaps they gathered once to delight in blossom,
   but after the children were killed
   there were no more buds.
3) Sir, laughter is bitter to the burned mouth.
4) A dream ago, perhaps. Ornament is for joy.
   All the bones were charred.
5) It is not remembered. Remember,
   most were peasants; their life
   was in rice and bamboo.
   When peaceful clouds were reflected in the paddies
   and the water buffalo stepped surely along terraces,
   maybe fathers told their sons old tales.
   When bombs smashed those mirrors
   there was time only to scream.
6) There is an echo yet
   of their speech which was like a song.
   It was reported their singing resembled
   the flight of moths in moonlight.
   Who can say? It is silent now.

Because in Vietnam the vision of a Burning Babe
is multiplied, multiplied,
                              the flesh on fire
not Christ's, as Southwell saw it, prefiguring
the Passion upon the Eve of Christmas,

but wholly human and repeated, repeated,
infant after infant, their names forgotten,
their sex unknown in the ashes,
set alight, flaming but not vanishing,
not vanishing as his vision but lingering,

cinders upon the earth or living on
moaning and stinking in hospitals three abed;

because of this my strong sight,
my clear caressive sight, my poet's sight I was given
that it might stir me to song,
is blurred.
              There is a cataract filming over
my inner eyes. Or else a monstrous insect
has entered my head, and looks out
from my sockets with multiple vision,

seeing not the unique Holy Infant
burning sublimely, an imagination of redemption,
furnace in which souls are wrought into new life,
but, as off a beltline, more, more senseless figures aflame.

And this insect (who is not there—
it is my own eyes do my seeing, the insect
is not there, what I see is there)
will not permit me to look elsewhere,

or if I look, to see except dulled and unfocused
the delicate, firm, whole flesh of the still unburned.

124

Tenebrae

(Fall of 1967)

Heavy, heavy, heavy, hand and heart.
We are at war,
bitterly, bitterly at war.

And the buying and selling
buzzes at our heads, a swarm
of busy flies, a kind of innocence.

Gowns of gold sequins are fitted,
sharp-glinting. What harsh rustlings
of silver moiré there are,
to remind me of shrapnel splinters.

And weddings are held in full solemnity
not of desire but of etiquette,
the nuptial pomp of starched lace;
a grim innocence.

And picnic parties return from the beaches
burning with stored sun in the dusk;
children promised a TV show when they get home
fall asleep in the backs of a million station wagons,
sand in their hair, the sound of waves
quietly persistent at their ears.
They are not listening.

Their parents at night
dream and forget their dreams.
They wake in the dark
and make plans. Their sequin plans
glitter into tomorrow.
They buy, they sell.

They fill freezers with food.
Neon signs flash their intentions
into the years ahead.

And at their ears the sound
of the war. They are
not listening, not listening.

Enquiry

You who go out on schedule
to kill, do you know
there are eyes that watch you,
eyes whose lids you burned off,
that see you eat your steak
and buy your girlflesh
and sell your PX goods
and sleep?
She is not old,
she whose eyes
know you.
She will outlast you.
She saw
her five young children
writhe and die;
in that hour
she began to watch you,
she whose eyes are open forever.

STAYING ALIVE

i

While the war drags on, always worse,
the soul dwindles sometimes to an ant
rapid upon a cracked surface;

lightly, grimly, incessantly
it skims the unfathomed clefts where despair
seethes hot and black.

ii

Children in the laundromat
waiting while their mothers fold sheets.
A five-year-old boy addresses
a four-year-old girl. 'When I say,
Do you want some gum? say *yes.*'
'Yes . . .' 'Wait!—Now:
Do you want some gum?'
'Yes!'   'Well yes means no,
so you can't have any.'
He chews. He pops a big, delicate bubble at her.

O language, virtue
of man, touchstone
worn down by what
gross friction . . .

        And,
' "It became necessary
to destroy the town to save it,"
a United States major said today.
He was talking about the decision
by allied commanders to bomb and shell the town
regardless of civilian casualties,
to rout the Vietcong.'

O language, mother of thought,
are you rejecting us as we reject you?

Language, coral island
accrued from human comprehensions,
human dreams,

you are eroded as war erodes us.

iii

To repossess our souls we fly
to the sea. To be reminded
of its immensity, and the immense sky
in which clouds move at leisure,
transforming their lives ceaselessly,
sternly, playfully.

*Today is the 65th day since de Courcy Squire, war-resister,
began her fast in jail. She is 18.*

And the sun
is warm bread, good to us, honest.
And the sand gives itself to our feet
or to our outstretched bodies,
hospitable, accommodating, its shells
unendingly at hand for our wonder.

*. . . arrested with 86 others Dec. 7. Her crime:
sitting down in front of a police wagon
momentarily preventing her friends from being
hauled to prison. Municipal Judge Heitzler
handed out 30-day suspended sentences to several others
accused of the same offense, but condemned
Miss Squire to 8 months in jail and fined her
$650. She had said in court 'I don't think there should be
roles like judge and defendant.'*

130

iv

Peace as grandeur. Energy
serene and noble. The waves
break on the packed sand,

butterflies take the cream o' the foam,
from time to time a palmtree lets fall
another dry branch, calmly.
                              The restlessness
of the sound of waves
transforms itself in its persistence
to that deep rest.
                    At fourteen
after measles my mother took me
to stay by the sea. In the austere presence

of Beachy Head we sat long hours
close to the tideline. She read aloud
from George Eliot, while I half-dozed
and played with pebbles. Or I read
to myself Richard Jefferies'
The Story of My Heart, which begins

in such majesty.
                  I was mean and grouchy
much of the time, but she forgave me,

and years later remembered
only the peace of that time.

The quiet there is
in listening.
              Peace could be

that grandeur, that dwelling
in majestic presence, attuned
to the great pulse.

131

The cocks crow all night
far and near. Hoarse with expectation.
And by day stumble red-eyed in the dust
where the heat flickers its lizard tongue.

In my dream the city
was half Berlin, half Chicago—
midwest German, Cincinnati perhaps,
where de Courcy Squire is.
There were many of us
jailed there, in moated fortresses—
five of them, with monosyllabic
guttural names. But by day
they led us through the streets,
dressed in our prisoners' robes—
smocks of brown holland—
and the people watched us pass
and waved to us, and gave us
serious smiles of hope.

Between us and the beach
a hundred yards of trees, bushes, buildings,
cut the breeze. But at the *verge*
of the salt flood, always
a steady wind, prevailing.

While we await your trial,
(and this is no dream) we are

free to come and go. To rise
from sleep and love and dreams about
ambiguous circumstance, and from
waking in darkness to cockcrow, and moving
deliberately (by keeping still) back into
morning sleep; to rise and float

into the blue day, the elaborate rustlings
of the palmtrees way overhead; to hover
with black butterflies at the lemon-blossom.
The sea awaits us; there are sweet oranges
on our plates; the city grayness has been
washed off our skins, we take pleasure
in each other's warmth of rosy brown.

vi

'Puerto Rico, Feb. 23, 1968.

                    . . . Some people, friends sincerely
concerned for us but who don't seem to understand what
it's really all about, apparently feel sorry for us because
Mitch has been indicted. One letter this morning said,
shyly and abruptly, after talking about quite unrelated mat-
ters, "My heart aches for you." Those people don't under-
stand that however boring the trial will be in some ways,
and however much of a distraction, as it certainly is, from
the things one's nature would sooner be engaged with, yet
it's quite largely a kind of pleasure too, a relief, a satisfac-
tion of the need to confront the war-makers and, in the
process, do something to wake up the bystanders.
        . . . Mitch and the others have a great deal of support,
people who think of them as spokesmen; they have good
lawyers, and have had and will have a lot of publicity of the
kind one hopes will be useful—I don't mean useful for their
case, saving them from going to jail, I mean useful towards
clarifying the issues, stopping the draft, helping to end the
war.'

    But something like a cramp
    of fury begins to form

(in the blue day, in the sweetness
of life we float in, allowed
this interim before the trial)
a cramp of fury at the mild,
saddened people whose hearts ache
not for the crimes of war,
the unspeakable—of which, then,
I won't speak—
and not for de Courcy Squire's
solitary passion
                    but for us.

Denied visitors, even her parents;
confined to a locked cell without running water
or a toilet.
           On January 29th, the 53rd day of her fast,
Miss Squire was removed to a hospital.
All the doctors would do was inform her that
the fast may cause her permanent brain injury.

'The sympathy of mild good folk,
a kind of latex from their leaves;
our inconvenience draws it out.

The white of egg without the yolk,
it soothes their conscience and relieves
the irritations of their doubt.'

. . . You see how it is—I am angry that they feel no outrage.
Their feeling flows in the wrong directions and at the wrong
intensity. And all I can bring forth out of my anger is a
few flippant rhymes. What I want to tell you—no, not you,
you understand it; what I want them to grasp is that though
I understand that Mitch may have to go to jail and that it
will be a hard time for him and for me, yet, because it's for

134

doing what we know we must do, that hardship is imaginable, encompassable, and a small thing in the face of the slaughter in Vietnam and the other slaughter that will come. And there is no certainty he will go to jail.'

And the great savage saints of outrage—
who have no lawyers,
who have no interim
in which to come and go,
for whom there is no world left—
their bodies rush upon the air in flames,
sparks fly, fragments of charred rag
spin in the whirlwind, a vacuum
where there used to be this monk or that,
Norman Morrison, Alice Hertz.

Maybe they are crazy. I know I could never
bring myself to injure my own flesh, deliberately.
And there are other models of behavior
to aspire to—A. J. Muste did not burn himself
but worked through a long life to make from outrage
islands of compassion others could build on.
Dennis Riordon, Bob Gilliam, how many others,
are alive and free in the jails. Their word is good,
language draws breath again in their *yes* and *no,*
true testimony of love and resistance.

But we need
the few who could bear no more,
who would try anything,
who would take the chance
that their deaths among the uncountable
masses of dead might be real to those who
don't dare imagine death.
Might burn through the veil that blinds
those who do not imagine the burned bodies
of other people's children.

We need them.
Brands that flare to show us
the dark we are in,
to keep us moving in it.

vii

To expand again, to plunge
our dryness into the unwearying source—

but not to forget.
Not to forget but to remember better.

We float in the blue day
darkly. We rest behind half-closed louvers,
the hot afternoon clouds up,
the palms hold still.

'I have a medical problem that can be cured'—
Miss Squire said last week when she was removed
from the city workhouse to Cincinnati General Hospital,
'I have a medical problem that can be cured
only by freedom.'

Puerto Rico, February–March, 1968

Part I

(October '68–May '69)

i

Revolution or death. Revolution or death.
Wheels would sing it
                         but railroads are obsolete,
we are among the clouds, gliding, the roar
a toneless constant.
                    Which side are you on?
Revolution, of course. Death is Mayor Daley.
This revolution has no blueprints, and
                    ('What makes this night different
                    from all other nights?')
is the first that laughter and pleasure aren't shot down in.

Life that
          wants to live.
                              (Unlived life
                              of which one can die.)
                    I want the world to go on
               unfolding. The brain
not gray except in death, the photo I saw
of prismatic radiance pulsing from live tissue.
               I see Dennis Riordon and de Courcy Squire,
               gentle David Worstell, intransigent Chuck Matthei
               blowing angel horns at the imagined corners.
               Jennie Orvino singing
               beatitudes in the cold wind
                              outside a Milwaukee courthouse.
I want their world—in which they already live,
they're not waiting for demolition and reconstruction.
                              'Begin here.'
Of course I choose
revolution.

ii

And yet, yes, there's the death
that's not the obscene sellout, the coprophiliac spasm
that smears the White House walls with its desensitized
                                        thumbs.

> Death lovely,
> whispering,
> *a drowsy numbness . . .*
>   *'tis not*
> *from envy of thy happy lot*
>   *lightwingéd dryad . . .*

Even the longest river . . .

Revolution or death. Love
aches me.   *. . . river*
winds somewhere to the sea.

iii

Shining of Lorie's hair, swinging
          alive, color of new copper—

who has died and risen.
'What am I doing here? I had died—'
(The nurses are frightened. The doctor
refuses to tell what happened those four hours.)
whose body at twenty-three is at war
within itself
trying to die again,

whose 'psychic energy' pulls her ten ways:
sculpture   poetry   painting
psychology   photography   teaching
cookery   love   Chinese philosophy
physics

          If she can live I can live.

iv

Trying one corner after another
to flag down a cab
                at last unthinking as one at last
                seems to see me,
                              I run into the traffic—
screech of brakes,
human scream, mine,
anger of drivers and shocked pedestrians
yelling at me!
                Is that how death is,
                    that poor, that trivial? I'm
not even frightened, only ashamed,
the driver almost refusing me,
scolding me half the way to the airport, I
strenuous to convince him I'm not
a habitual public danger.
So close to death and thinking only
of being forgiven by strangers.

v

Gliding among clouds.   The will to live
pulses.   Radiant emanations
of living tissue, visible only
to some photo-eye we know
sees true because mind's dream-eye,
inward gage, confirms it.
                Confirmation,
a sacrament.

                Around the Fish
(it's reproduced here in the magazine the air-hostess gives me)
                    rearranges itself as *Around the—*
                    Nature of Death, is it? *How*
                    to Live, What to Do?

after yet another return home,
first thing I see is a picture postcard
that stood on the windowledge all summer,
somehow not seen. An Assyrian relief. The wings
(as I look at the words I've written, 'gliding among clouds')
draw me to pick it up and examine it:
a sturdy muscular being it shows,
thick-bearded, heavy-sandalled;
wings made for crossing from world to world.
His hair is bound with a wreath;
in his left hand he grips
a thickstemmed plant bearing five blossoms.

Who sent him?

I turn the card over—ah! at once
I know the hand—Bill Rose's. This was his message to me,
six months ago, unanswered. Is now the newly dead—
less than three weeks—trying to speak to me
one last time?

> How to live and the will to live,
> what was recalled to me of those
> rainbow pulsations some Russian scientist
> discovered,
> the choosing
> always before me now that sings itself
> quietly, *revolution or death*

>> cluster about some center
>> unknown, shifting but retaining—
>> snowflake forms in a kaleidescope—
>> a character that throughout all transformations
>> reveals them connatural.

And to that cluster

this winged genie from Nimrud
now adds himself,
last sign from a friend whose life
failed him in some way long before death:

a man my age
a man deeply dissatisfied
as he told me once.

           'It came on very suddenly; he
found out at the end of the summer that nothing could be
done for him, so to make the waiting easier, he decided to
go on teaching. But within a few weeks of that decision, he
was dead.'
      And someone else writes: 'Mr Rose was such a
lone figure; he lived alone; you mostly saw him alone; and
that's what's so hard to take: he died alone. I never knew
him except by sight.'

Is there anything
I write any more that is not
elegy?
      Goldengrove
is unleaving all around me; I live
in goldengrove; all day
yesterday and today the air has been filled
with that hesitant downwardness;
the marigolds, the pumpkin, must be sought out
to be seen, the grass
is covered with that cloth, the roads'
margins illuminated.

vi

Learned—not for the first time—my 'roots in the
19th century' put me
                out of touch.

Born in the '20's, but a late child, my parents' memories
pivoting on their first meeting, Constantinople, 1910, and
returning into the '90's. Reading, I went straight from
Grimm and Andersen to the 19th-century novel. Until the

war—1939—there was a muffin-man who came by in foggy
winter dusks, tea-time, ringing his bell, his wares balanced
on his head according to the mysteries of his trade as if
Dickens were still alive—
The 'Ode to a Nightingale' was the first and only poem I
ever learned by heart. Thus, when I wrote, translating,
'*purged* of legend,' the reader's thought was of Stalin, while
my intention was something more graphic than the literal
'cured'—

and again when I said the sun approached
'to study the flower,' the reader—

>   to whom I would give
>   all that arms can hold, eyes
>   encompass—

alas, thought of a tedious process,
grade-points, term-papers—while I had meant 'study—e.g.,

>   I study your face intently
>   but its secret eludes me,'
>   or, 'he took her hand and studied
>   the strong fingers, the veins,
>   the curious ring.'

Without a terrain in which, to which, I belong,
language itself is my one home, my Jerusalem,

yet time and the straddled ocean
undo me, maroon me,
(roadblocks, the lines down)—

>   I choose
>   revolution but my words

often already don't reach forward

>   into it—
>   (perhaps)

>   Whom I would touch
>   I may not,

whom I may
I would
but often do not.

My diction marks me
untrue to my time;
change it, I'd be
untrue to myself.
                    I study
a face intently.
Learning.
Beginning to learn.
And while
        I study,
                O, in that act
of passionate attention
A drowsy numbness
pains my sense.
            Too happy in thy happiness.
Love of living.   *That wants to live.*   *Unlived life.*
whisper
of goldengrove . . .

i

Last of October, light thinning
towards the cold. Deep shadow.

Yellow honey, the ridge, a grove 'thrown into relief,'
of tamaracks, lurid, glamorous
upon the breast of
moving darkness, clouds thick with
gunmetal blue.
It becomes
November without one's knowing it.
Broad rays from southwest-by-west
single out one by one
the fixed parts of earthscape.

And into the first snowstorm   (marooned)
the lines down
no phone
no lights
no heat
gastank for cooking about to give out
car stuck in the driveway.

        We find candles.
        We light up the woodstove which was all we
        used to have anyway, till a few weeks back.

ii

A fly I thought dead
on its back on the windowsill,
grayed, shrivelled,

slowly waves.
            Yes, what would be its right arm
dreamily moves—out—in—out again
twice, three times.
            It seems
flies dream in dying.

iii

Four p.m.—pleasure
in exercise
in air,
in sound of brook
under and out from
thin ice

pleasure
of chest and shoulders
pushing air that's
not cold enough to hurt.

Jumping
into snowbank—
no sound—

pleasure—

But to the eye
terror of a kind:

black-and-white photo world
not night yet
but at four p.m.
no light we know

hemlock and cedar a toneless black,
snowtufted trunks and boughs
black, sky white, birches
whiter, snow
infinitely whiter: all things
muted: deprived
of color, as if
color were utterance.
A terror
as of eclipse.
The whites graying.

iv

George told me, and then I read it in Beckett,
Proust had a bad memory,
                              the only kind worth having,
Beckett argues: there's no remembrance
                    and so no revelation,
   for those Admirable, terrifying, unimaginable Crichtons
   who don't disremember nothing, keep
   the whole works in mind.
No pain. No sharp stabs of recall. No revelation.

I stretch in luxury; knowledge of the superb badness
of my memory gives me a sense of having thick fur,
a tail, and buried somewhere
a sweet bone, rotten, enticing . . .

What pain! What sharp stabs of recall! What revelations!
The black taste of life, the music
angel tongues buzz when my paws nuzzle it
out into light!

v

Again to hold—'capture' they say—
moments and their processions in palm
of mind's hand.
                    Have you ever,
in stream or sea,
                    felt the silver of fish
pass through your hand-hold? not to stop it,
block it from going onward, but feel it
move in its wave-road?
                         To make
                    of song a chalice,
                         of Time,
                    a communion wine.

Part II

Can't go further.
If there's to be a
second part, it's not
a going beyond, I'm
still here.

To dig down,
to re-examine.

.   .   .   .

What is the revolution I'm driven
to name, to live in? —that now roars,
a toneless constant, now
sings itself?

        It's in the air: no air
                to breathe without
        scent of it,
             pervasive:
        odor of snow,
              freshwater,
                  stink of dank
              vegetation recomposing.

—Yet crisply
the moon's risen,
full, complete.
Secret uprising (last time I looked,
        surely not long since,
        dark was
        as complete).
The snowfields have been
taken over

(glistening crust of ice upon snow
in driftwaves, curves of stilled
wind-caress, bare to the moon
in silence of adoration).

                    If it were so for us!
                    But that's the moon's world.

                    .   .   .   .

Robert reminds me *revolution*
implies the circular: an exchange
of position, the high
brought low, the low
ascending, a revolving,
an endless rolling of the wheel. The wrong word.
We use the wrong word. A new life
isn't the old life in reverse, negative of the same photo.
But it's the only
word we have . . .

                    .   .   .   .

Chuck Matthei
travels the country
                    a harbinger.
(He's 20. His golden beard was pulled and clipped
        by a Wyoming sheriff, but no doubt has grown

                                                again

        though he can't grow knocked-out teeth.
        He wears sneakers even in winter,
            to avoid animal-hide; etc.)
And on his journeyings bears
my poem 'A Man'
to prisoners in the jails.
                    Of Mitch I wrote it,

even before anyone heard
the voice he
brought to song.
But Chuck has found in it
a message for all who resist war,
disdain to kill,
try to equate
'human' with 'humane.'
(And if his intransigeance
brings us another despair
and we call it 'another form of aggression,'
don't we confess—
wishing he had a sense of humor—
our own extremity?)

'Living a life' the poem begins.
'—the beauty of deep lines
dug in your cheeks'
and ends,
'you pick out
your own song from the uproar,

line by line,
and at last throw back
your head and sing it.'
Next on the mimeograph follows:
'THERE IS ONLY AS MUCH PEACE AS THERE ARE
PEACEFUL PEOPLE'
(A. J. Muste)
Then Chuck has written:
This is your only life—live it well!

No one man can bring about a social change—
    but each man's life is a whole and necessary part of his
    society,
    a necessary step in any change,
    and a powerful example of the possibility of life
    for others.

Let all of our words and our actions speak the possibility of
peace and cooperation between men.
Too long have we used the excuse:
'I believe in peace, but that other man does not—when
he lays down his arms, then I will follow.'

Which of us deserves to wait to be the last good man
on earth; how long will we wait if all of us wait?

Let each man begin a one-man revolution of peace and
mutual aid—so that there is at least that much peace . . .
a beginning; . . .

A beginning.
Where shall we
begin?
Can't go
further.

       Time, says the old Canon,
in Denis Saurat's *Death and the Dreamer,*
       is not a sequence,
       as man's simplicity thinks, but radiates
out from a center
         every direction,
         all
           dimensions
             (pulsations, as from living cells,
radiant—

      . . . .

May 14th, 1969—Berkeley
Went with some of my students to work in the People's
Park. There seemed to be plenty of digging and gardening
help so we decided, as Jeff had his truck available, to shovel
up the garbage that had been thrown into the west part of
the lot and take it out to the city dump.

151

O happiness
in the sun! Is it
that simple, then,
to live?
—crazy rhythm of
scooping up barehanded
(all the shovels already in use)
careless of filth and broken glass
—scooping up garbage together
poets and dreamers studying
joy together, clearing
refuse off the neglected, newly recognized,
humbly waiting ground, place, locus, of what could be our
New World even now, our revolution, one and one and
one and one together, black children swinging, green
guitars, that energy, that music, no one
                    telling anyone what to do,
                    everyone doing,

      each leaf of
      the new grass near us
      a new testament . . .

Out to the dump:
acres of garbage glitter and stink in wild sunlight, gulls
float and scream in the brilliant sky,
polluted waters bob and dazzle, we laugh, our arms ache,
                    we work together
shoving and kicking and scraping to empty our truckload
                    over the bank
even though we know
the irony of adding to the Bay fill, the System has us there—
but we love each other and return to the Park.

Thursday, May 15th
At 6 a.m. the ominous zooming, war-sound, of helicopters
breaks into our sleep.

To the Park:
ringed with police.
Bulldozers have moved in.
Barely awake, the people—
those who had made for each other
a green place—
begin to gather at the corners.

Their tears fall on sidewalk cement.
The fence goes up, twice a man's height.
Everyone knows (yet no one yet
believes it) what all shall know
this day, and the days that follow:
now, the clubs, the gas,
bayonets, bullets. The War
comes home to us . . .

. . . .

WHAT PEOPLE CAN DO

1. Be in the streets—they're ours!
2. Report any action you have witnessed or been involved in that should be broadcast to keep the people informed. Especially call to report the location of any large groups of people, so those people who have been separated may regroup . . .
3. The Free Church and Oxford Hall medical aid stations need medical supplies, especially:
   —gauze pads
   —adhesive tape
   —plastic squeeze bottles.
4. PLEASE do not go to the Free Church unless you have need to.
5. Photographers and filmmakers: Contact Park Media Committee.
6. Bail money will be collected at tables outside the COOP grocery stores:
   —Telegraph Ave. store: Monday
   —University Ave. store: Tuesday
   —Shattuck Ave. store: Wed. & Thurs.
7. BRING YOUR KITE AND FLY IT. Use nylon strings. Fly it when you are with a crowd. A helicopter cannot fly too near flying kites.
8. Be your brothers' and sisters' keeper.
9. Take care.

'change is now
change is now
things that seem to be solid are not'

The words came through, transistor
turned up loud. The music, the beat,
lost now, but
the words hang on.

Revolution: a crown of tree
            raises itself out of the heavy
            flood.
                    A branch lifts
                    under null skies' weight
            pushes against
            walls of air, flashing
            clefts in it.

The floodwaters
stir, mud
swirls to the surface.

            A hand, arm,
            lifts in the crawl—
            hands, arms, intricate
                    upflashing—
                            a sea full of swimmers!
                    their faces' quick steady
                    lift for air—

Maybe what seems
evanescent is solid.

Islands
step out of the waves on rock feet.

i   **At the Justice Department**
     November 15, 1969

Brown gas-fog, white
beneath the street lamps.
Cut off on three sides, all space filled
with our bodies.
        Bodies that stumble
in brown airlessness, whitened
in light, a mildew glare,
        that stumble
hand in hand, blinded, retching.
Wanting it, wanting
to be here, the body believing it's
dying in its nausea, my head
clear in its despair, a kind of joy,
knowing this is by no means death,
is trivial, an incident, a
fragile instant.   Wanting it, wanting
        with all my hunger this anguish,
        this knowing in the body
the grim odds we're
up against, wanting it real.
Up that bank where gas
curled in the ivy, dragging each other
up, strangers, brothers
and sisters.   Nothing
will do but
to taste the bitter
taste. No life
other, apart from.

156

ii   Gandhi's Gun (and Brecht's Vow)

Vessels of several
shapes and sizes—

bowls, pots,
a tall vase

and the guitar's
waiting body:

forms drawn
by a hand's
energy.

       'Never

       run away from the stormcenter.

       Cultivate

       cool courage, die without killing—'

Strong orange, deep
oil-pastel green

but at the center, strange
upstroke of black

stronger, deeper
than all.

       —'but if one has not

       that courage'—

(or singing, *'Keiner
oder Alle, Alles
oder Nichts!'*)
       —'cultivate

    the art of killing and being killed

    rather than in a cowardly manner

        to flee from danger.'

Vessels, counterparts
of the human; primal
vessel of music

towards which like a rifle
that harsh stroke blackly
points upward

would fail, fall from their whirling
dance, without

the terror patiently
poised there,

ultimate focus.

iii   The Year One

Arn says it's
the Year one.

And I
know such violent

revolution has ached
my marrowbones, my

soul changing
its cells, my

cracked heart tolling
such songs of

unknown morning-star
ecstatic anguish, the clamor

of unquenched desire's
radiant decibels shattering

the patient wineglasses
set out by private history's ignorant

quiet hands,   —I keep
enduring such pangs of giving

birth or being
born,
      I dream

maybe he's right.

Looking for the Devil Poems

'Tell Denise to write about the devil.'

i

Tell Sam
it is (perhaps) the devil
made me so goddamned strong

that I have made myself
(almost)
numb,
almost unable
to feel in me
(for now)
the beautiful outreaching of desire.

And tell him
it is perhaps the devil
inserted these parenthetical
qualifications.

ii

It's the devil
swarms into 'emptiness'
not
    waiting
        until it slowly
        as a jar let stand
        at fountain's edge, fills,
        drop by drop,
but busily, as if not water
but flies buzzing were what
'emptiness' were to hold.

160

iii

Looking for the devil I walked
down Webster St. and across on
Cottage St. and down
Sumner to Maverick Square
and saw
3 dogs nosing the green plastic
   garbage bags on the sidewalk,
5 children screaming cheerfully together, sliding
                          upon a strip of gray ice,
1 simpleton (Webster St.'s own) who waved and called
                              'Hi!' to me,
4 elderly Italian peasant women (separately)
                       lugging home groceries
   in big shopping bags, their faces solemn
                   as at some ritual,
2 twelve-year-old girls in cheap maxicoats,
10 more or less silent teen-aged boys
              in groups of 3 or 4 standing
   on several corners, collars up, seeming
              to wait for something which
   was not about to happen,
2 middle-aged bookies, one wearing
   a seedy chesterfield—the same guys I saw
   one day at the Buffalo Meat Market ordering
   some big steaks, but today
   down on their luck—

and no doubt some other persons, but these
were all I noticed:
and in none of these
could I discern the devil
(under the sullen January sky) nor was the devil,
surely, the east wind
blowing garbage out of the bags after
the dogs succeeded in ripping them,
nor was the devil the ugly
dogshit innocently smeared on the pavement.

Was he then
my eyes that searched for him?
Or was he the inexorable
smog of tedium that we breathed,
I and all these, even
the children at play, even, quite possibly, the dogs?

Or was he
the toneless ignorance all that I saw
had of itself?

v   **Today**

Just feeling human
the way a cloud's a cloud
tinged with blue or
walking slow across the sky or
hastening,
but not a Thursday cloud
formed for the anxious glance of Thursday people,
simply a cloud, whose particles
may fall Tuesday, just as well,
on anyone's springy hair, on any
taciturn winter buds it chooses
and no one say no. Human,
free for the day from roles assigned,
each with its emblem
cluttering the right hand,
scroll of words in the left.
Human, a kind of element, a fire,
an air, today.
Floating up to you I enter, or you
enter me. Or imagine
a house without doors,
open to sun or snowdrifts.

162

vi   **Casa Felice (I)**

Getting back into
ordinary gentle morning, tide
        wavelessly dreaming in,
            silent gulls at ease on wheatsheaf sandbars—

Off the limb of
desperation
            I drop
            plumb into peace for a day—

it's
    not easy.
            But easier—
                    O blesséd
                    blue!
            —than fear and reason
            supposed of late.

vii   **Casa Felice (II)**

Richard, if you were here
would you too be peaceful?

(I am angry
all of the time, not just sometimes,
you said. *We must*
smash the state.
Smash the state.)

If you were here
for these two days at Casa
Felice, if you were here and listened
to the almost soundless tide
incoming,
        what would it say to you?

Would you feel new
coldness towards me
because this April morning, gentle light
on the unglittering sea and pale sands,
I am not angry and not tense?

viii   Revolutionary

When he said
'Your struggle is my struggle'
a curtain was pushed away.

A curtain was pushed away revealing
an open window
and beyond that

an open country.
For the first time I knew it was actual.
I was indoors still

but the air from fields
beyond me touched my face.

It was a country
of hilly fields, of many
shadows and rivers.

The thick heavy dark
curtain had hidden
a world from me;

curtain of sorrow, world
where far-off I see
people moving—

struggling to move, as I
towards my window
struggle, burdened but not

each alone. They move
out in that air together
where I too

will be moving,
not alone.

ix   'I Thirst'

Beyond the scaffolding set up for
TV cameras, a long way
from where I sit among 100,000 reddening
white faces,
            is a big wooden cross:

and strapped upon it, turning
his head from side to side in pain
in the 90-degree shadeless Washington midafternoon
May 9th, 1970,
            a young black man.

'We must *not* be angry, we must
L-O-O-O-V-E!' Judy Collins
bleats loud and long into the P.A. system,

but hardly anyone claps, and no one
shouts *Right On*.
            That silence cheers me.
Judy, understand:
there comes a time when only anger
is love.

Part III

*(Europe after 10 years; England after
20 years; summer of 1970)*

i

Silver summer light of Trieste early evening

>   (a silver almost gold
>   almost grey).

Caffè,
little cup
black and sweet.

>   The waiter
>   tall and benevolent
>   gives some change to a wanderer
>   (not a beggar,
>   he has a pack,
>   is maybe 30 and
>   no taller than a boy of 11).
>   Almost weeping with weariness.
>   Stands to gaze at a green plant.
>   Droops.
>   Sinks to the pavement.
>   The waiter
>   gently sends him across the street
>   to a marble bench set in the church wall.

'Where is he from, that man?'
A shrug—'É Italiano . . .'

Maybe from Sicily. Later I pause
to watch him
curled like a tired child on the stone.

·

Caffè, another
sweet and black
little cup.

Cop-out, am I,
or merely,
    as the day fades

        (and Amerika
        far away
        tosses in fever)

on holiday?

ii

            And David said
            in England

            What's a cop-out? Is it
            the same as
            opting out?

            And I said
            Yes, but
            opting out sounds like
            cool choice

            and copping-out
            means fear and weakness

but he said
No,
we mean that too.

iii

Strange, a rusty freight train's passing
between the cafés and the sea
(a long train of cars
veiled in old Europe's dust—maybe
they've shuttled up and down the Adriatic
since before the War, and inland,
anywhere)

cutting between the sidewalk tables
              and the view
to no one's surprise but mine

and when they've gone by
the dim sea
has vanished,

vague silver
tarnished to blue;

points of amber
show where the suburbs
drift over down-grey hills.

iv

Summer dusk,
Triestino,
deep blue now.

The port, its commerce:
a few gold bars
broken upon the water.

A ship from Genoa
riding at anchor.
Port light, starboard.

The sky   the water
     warm   blue   blurred.

v

On the broad Riva
among young couples
taking the air with their babies

men still prowl as they used to,
laughably. Buona sera. Buona sera, Signorina.
                    (That spring of '48, the weeks
                    alone in Florence, waiting for Mitch.
                    And I used to talk to the Israeli terrorist,
                    if that's what he was, in the Pensione,
                    but the Signora told me to watch out for him,
                    a young bride should watch out.)
                                        Buona sera.
No sexual revolution here, no Women's Lib.
That's the third car to slow down.
        (The difference is, more cars,
        new ones too, I see.)
Buona sera, signorina. Each driver
leans out, affable.
                    Evidently
I must give up my
slow stroll.

(And in me the difference
is, I'm not scared,
I find them only foolish, they're
in my way.

But do they spend every evening
cruising?   No whores around,
too early maybe. Whom do they
hope for?)

I turn briskly along a one-way street.
In the hotel lobby, *terza classe,*
a young man, thickly handsome,
looks at me over the *Corriere della Sera*
and jumps up to follow me
but I get upstairs to my door and in and
shut it, just as his mechanical shadow
precedes him into the corridor.

'Honestly! I *ask* you!'
some English voice laughs in my head.

Buona notte.

vi

Back in Boston a month ago I wrote:

'At my unhappiest,
like the next guy, I want

oblivion

but even when
a couple of sleeping pills or
total immersion in an almost-boring fiction

at last succeed in
shutting my eyes and
whatever torment ails me shuts off
and I get what I wanted

oblivion,

I don't want it for long.
I don't know
how to be mute, or deaf, or blind,
for long, but
wake and plunge into next day
talking, even if I say *yesterday* when I mean *tomorrow*,
listening, even if what I'm hearing
has the *approaching* sound of terror,
seeing, even if the morning light
and all it reveals appear
pathetic in ignorance,
like unconscious heroes trapped on film,
raised shadows about to descend and smash their skulls.

And when I'm not
unhappy but am
alone, then specially some hunger for revelation
keeps me up half the night
wandering from book to music to painting to book,
reluctant
to give any time at all to oblivion—

only the hope of memorable dreams
at last luring me
exhausted to bed.'

Now I can barely remember what it is
to want oblivion. 'The dreamy lamps
of stonyhearted Oxford Street'—
de Quincy wandered
in hopeless search beneath them,

Olga rushed back and forth
for years beneath them, working
in her way for Revolution
and I too in my youth
knew them and was lonely, an ignorant girl.
But I forget anguish
as I forget joy

returning after 20 years
to 'merry London' as to a nest.

(Say what one will,
know what one must
of Powell, of the farm hand's
£13 a week—and they vote
Tory—yet

there is a gentleness
lost in anxious Amerika—

it's in the way
three young workmen in the Tube
smiled to each other
admiring their day-off purchases,
new shirts—

it's in the play-talk
of children, without irony:
not *cool*, not
joshing each other,

and in the way
men and women of any age maintain
some expectation of love,

(not pickups, but love) and so
remain beautiful:

there
　　　'in merry London, my most kindly nurse,
　　that to me gave this life's first native source'

　　my friends whose lives
　　　have been knit with mine a quarter century
　are not impaled on the spears of the cult of youth).
Aie, violent Amerika, aie, dynamic
deathly-sick America, of whose energy,
in whose fever, in whose wild
cacophonous music I have lived
and will live,

　　what gentleness, what kindness
of the *private life* I left, unknowing,

and gained instead the tragic, fearful
knowledge of *present history,*
of doom. . . 'Imagination of disaster. . .life
ferocious and sinister'. . .

·

　　　But shall I forget
　euphoria on the bus from
　Trafalgar Square to Kings Cross?
　　　　What a laugh,
　there's nothing so great about Kings Cross,

　but life is in me, a love for
　what happens, for
　the surfaces that are their own
　interior life, yes, the
　Zen buildings! the
　passing of the
　never-to-be-seen-again
　faces! I bless

173

every stone I see, the
'happy genius' not of my household perhaps

but of my solitude. . .

vii

Two hours after reaching Rijeka
(that once was Fiume)
I'm drinking *vinjak* with five Sudanese.

(Four days ago I was in Dorset. We drank
cider and walked in the rain.)

Jugoslavia still unknown, mysterious,
slow train-ride, rocky fields in heat haze
                          and now
a roomful of subtle
black faces!
They refill my glass and give me
The Baghdad Observer: 'Al-Ali Reviews
Revolutionary Achievements.' I give them
the news about Bobby Seale.

I ask one for a towel,
he gives me his own.

I help clear the ash trays,
they say, No, that's *our* work.

They sing, and drum on whatever comes to hand,
(one makes a bell of knife and glass)
and two of them dance.
                          Outside,

oleanders astir in folds of
dense night.

To Abubakar I gave
my Panther button, the yellow one
with the great Black Cat emerging
in power from behind bars.

they read, and repeated it
to each other in Arabic.

And he gave me
a photo of turbanned dancers
and one of a bridge crossing the Blue Nile.

Abubakar, gat-toothed
like me.   'They say it's lucky,'
I told him, 'and means you will journey
very far.'

        In that room I knew the truth of what José
Yglesias writes, in his book on revolutionary Cuba that I'm
reading here on this Adriatic island 3 days later: he had
been to a film, a good one but these Cuban country people
took it with 'none of the tension, the concentration there
would have been in New York. . . . Their presence made me
see that for all its artistry . . . it was a false picture of life:
[they] knew that the easy-going goodness of people was
missing from it, that it allowed no avenue for joy, such as
they knew exists as soon as any bar to its enjoyment is let
down. Nor does it take a revolution to know this, just a bit
of living.'

And I remembered the time, just a few months ago,
a bitter March night in Boston, I went to see *Rock Around
the Clock* with Richard and Boat and someone else from
their collective, that was the same, gave me the same joy as
this roomful of friends, there was the same sense of generosity
and good humor, but more frantic, a sense of stolen time, of
pleasure only taken in recognition of desperate need *some-
times* to let up, a respite from the chills of fevered Amerika—

               and here a leisure,
               a courtesy unhurried
      as if the bare student pad
      were full of flowers, jasmine,
      roses . . .
            Selah.
Abubakar—I gave him
my promise to find out in what country
he might enter medical school:
        'If I have to, I'll go
        to a capitalist country.'
And he (20, slender, beardless,
gentle, and warm to touch as a nectarine
ripe in the sun)

asked for and gave
a kind of love.

viii

After the American lava
has cooled and set in new forms,
will you Americans have

              more peace and less hope?
wonders Sasha, socialist,
            ('but not a Party member')

(We have not been asked, adds his wife

primly, the smallest smile
whisking across her elegant, honest face).

Is that what *you* have—
peace without hope?
                    I counter;

(and it seems perhaps
that *is* what they have
—at least,
none of the fervor here
that blazes in Cuban cane fields).

I swim out
over sharp rocks, sea urchins,
thinking, When I go back,

when I go back into the writhing lava,
will I rejoice in
fierce hope, in
wanhope, in
'righteous' pleasurable hope?

              Could struggle be enough, even
              without hope?

                    For that I'm not
                    enough a puritan. Or not yet.
                    (Richard might say: history intervenes
                    to weld endurance, revolution
              builds character—
                        but he is young,
              a young dreamer, wilful, stern).
                                And peace—
I think I have
            not *hope* for it,
only a longing . . .

But on a hill in Dorset
    while the bells of Netherbury
    pealed beyond the grove of
    great beeches,
        and Herefords,
    white starred on tawny ample brows,
    grazed, slow, below us,
           only days ago,
Bet said:
There was a dream I dreamed always
over and over,

a tunnel
and I in it, distraught

and great dogs blocking
each end of it

and I thought I must
always go on
dreaming that dream,
trapped there,

but Mrs. Simon listened
and said

why don't you sit down
in the middle of the tunnel
quietly:

imagine yourself
quiet and intent sitting there,
not running from blocked
exit to blocked exit.

Make a place for yourself
in the darkness
and wait there. *Be* there.

The dogs
will not go away.
They must be transformed.

Dream it that way.
Imagine.

Your being, a fiery stillness,
is needed to TRANSFORM
the dogs.

And Bet said to me:
Get down into your well,

it's your well

go deep into it

into your own depth as into a poem.

'Let Us Sing Unto the Lord a New Song'

There's a pulse in Richard
that day and night says
revolution   revolution   revolution

and another
not always heard:

poetry   poetry

rippling through his sleep,
a river pulse.

Heart's fire
breaks the chest almost,
flame-pulse,
revolution:

and if its beat
falter
life itself
shall cease.

Heart's river,
living water,
poetry:

and if that pulse
grow faint
fever shall parch the soul, breath
choke upon ashes.

But when their rhythms
mesh
then though the pain of living
never lets up

the singing begins.

i Report

I went back.
Daily life
is not lava.
        It is
a substance that expands and contracts, a rhythm
different from the rhythm of history,
though history is made of the same
minutes and hours.
                Tony writes from Ohio:
                'An atomistic bleakness drags on students this fall
                after the fiery fusion of last spring.'

Airplane life: the fall for me
spent like a wildgoose that has lost
the migrating flock and lost
the sense of where the south is—
zigzagging—'gliding among clouds.'

England, back there in summer, and especially
the two Davids, turned out to be home: but my literal
home, these rooms, this desk, these small
objects of dailiness each with its history,
books, photos, and in the kitchen
the old breadknife from Ilford that says
Bread Knife on its blade—the least details—
are what pull me. No, it's not true that I'm
a defective migrant, I know as I fly
where I long to be. But the wind blows me
off course.

(Bromige writes: 'I recall the muffin man
too, and the naphtha lamps, I think they were, in the open-
air market, High Rd. Kilburn, after early December dark.
Now I sit up here on a California hillside. This difficulty of
what resonance has the language, for you, for me,—I need
to take up but the push and shove of events (that's a telling
phrase of Merleau-Ponty's!) has me, and meanwhile I go on
writing poems sometimes like shouting down a deep well.'
             Those are the same lamps
             of my dream of Olga—the eel or cockle stand,
             she in the flare caught, a moment, her face
             painted, clownishly, whorishly. Suffering.

'It's your own well.
Go down
into its depth.'

ii   Happiness

Two nights dancing (Workingmen's Dead)
with someone of such grace and goodness, happiness
made real in his true smile,
                      that it has seemed
I know now forever:
                      The reason for happiness is,
                      happiness exists.
Good Day Sunshine. The moon's vast aureole
of topaz was complete;
                      utterly still;
                              a covenant,
its terms unknown. / Waving arms! Swaying!
                              The whirling of the dance!

183

Soon after
more (but not deeper) depth of joy
was given me at the show of Zen paintings.
                    Camus wrote:
        'I discovered inside myself, even in the very midst of
        winter, an invincible summer.'
Again—
          as in the act of clearing garbage off the land
together with those I loved,
and later dodging with them
                              the swinging clubs of the cops,
living
in that momentary community—
again happiness
astonished me, so easy, 'amazing grace.'
Easy as the undreamed
dreamlike reality
of Abubakar and his friends.

But before this
came the death of Judy. Yes,
Judy had killed herself a full two weeks
before my hours of dancing began,
I found out the night I read to raise money
for the Juche Revolutionary Bookstore,

iii   Two from the Fall Death-News

and still I've not begun the poem,
the one she asked for ('If you would write me a poem
I could live for ever'—postmarked
the night she died, October twenty-ninth.)
I've begun though
to gather up fragments of it,
fragments of her: the heavy tarnished
pendant I don't wear,

the trapped dandelion seed in its transparent cube,
three notched green stones for divination, kept
                                    in green velvet,
a set of the *Daily Californian* for all the days
of the struggle for the People's Park,
a thick folder of her letters,
and now (come with the Christmas mail, packed
in a pink cosmetic box grotesquely labelled,
        'The Hope Chest'),
four cassettes recording (or so they are marked,
I've not played them) her voice speaking to me . . .

Revolution or death. She chose
as her life had long foretold. I can't lose her,
for I don't love her. In all her carefully kept
but unreread letters, all I remember sharply is the green
cold of the water in the deep pool she evoked,
the rock pool said to be bottomless,
where as a young girl she swam naked, diving
over and over, seeking
to plumb its roaring silence.

               •   •   •   •   •   •   •

                    But Grandin, he could have lived!
His death, a year ago, hits me now,
reading his poems, stitched into order before he too
stopped himself.
               Rage and awe
shake me.
And the longing to have spoken
long hours with him, to have gone
long walks with him beside rivers—
all I don't feel
for Judy, who in some fashion loved me,
lived through (for an hour, for recurring instants)
towards Grandin, to whom when he was alive
I was peripheral, as he to me . . .

185

'By the post house · windblown reed-fronds.
In some city tavern you dance the *Wild Mulberry Branch*.'
Rollicking, eyes flashing.   I resent your death
as if it were accidental.
          'Now snowstorms will fill the lands west of the Huai.
          I remember last year · broken candlelight upon
                              travelling-clothes.'
Last I heard of you, you were 'feeling better,'
up in some ghost town out West . . .
                                        ¶ feel life in your words,
tortured, savage.
                        Further away than 17th-century China,
nearer than my hand, you smashed
the world in the image of yourself, smashed
the horror of a world lonely Judy,
          silently plunging forever
into her own eyes' icy green, never even saw;
you raged bursting with life into death.

iv   **Daily Life**

Dry mouth,
              dry nostrils.
Dry sobs, beginning
abruptly, continuing
briefly,
          ending.
                  The heart
dragging back sand through steelblue veins,
scraping it back out into the arteries: and they take it.
Living in the gray desert and
getting used to it.   Years ago, Juan wrote:
'We can never forget ourselves, and our problems involve
others and deform them.'
                  And Hopkins:
          'Sorrow's springs are the same.'

186

Then rainbow day comes in flashing
off the snow-roofs. By afternoon, slogging
through falling snow,
yellow snowlight, traffic slowed to
carthorse pace,
                    exhilaration, East Boston
doubling for London.
                    I'm frivolous.
                              I'm alone.
                                        I'm Miriam
(in *Pilgrimage*) fierce with joy
                              in a furnished room near Euston.
I'm the Tailor of Gloucester's cat.
                              I live in one day
a manic-depressive's year.
                    I like
                              my boots, I like
the warmth of my new long coat. Last winter
running through Cambridge with Boat and Richard, afraid of
                                        the ice they
slid on fearlessly—I must have been cold all winter
without knowing it, in my short light coat.
Buffalo Meat Market offers me a drink, (Strega),
                              I lug home
the ham for Christmas Eve, life
whirls its diamond sparklers before me.
Yes, I want
          revolution, not death: but I don't
care about survival, I refuse
to be provident, to learn automechanics,
                    karate,
                    soybean cookery,
                    or how to shoot.
          O gray desert,
          I inhabit your mirages,
          palace after palace. . .
                    pineforest. . .
                    palmgrove. . .

Judy ignored the world outside herself,
Grandin was flooded by it.
There is no suicide in our time
unrelated to history, to whether
each before death had listened to the living, heard
the cry, 'Dare to struggle,
                    dare to win.'
heard and not listened, listened and turned away.

And I? 'Will struggle without hope
            be enough?' I was asking
on a sunny island in summer.
                                Now in midwinter
not doing much to struggle, or striving mainly
to get down into my well in hope
that force may gather in me
                    from being still in the grim
                    middle of the tunnel . . .
(And meanwhile Richard and Neil in their collectives
get down to it: get into work: food co-ops, rent strikes;
and 'Jacob and Lily' create
an active freedom in 'open hiding';
and Mitch has finished his book, 'a tool
for the long revolution.')
                            (And meanwhile Robert
                        sees me as Kali! No,
                I am not Kali, I can't sustain for a day
that anger.
            'There comes
                    a time
                        when only anger
                                    is love'—
I wrote it, but know such love
only in flashes.

                    And the love that streams
towards me daily, letters and poems, husband and child,
sings . . .)
                              Mayakovsky wrote,
                              in the 3-stepped lines that Williams
                              must have seen and learned from,

'Life
      must be
                    started quite anew,
when you've changed it,
                              then
                              the singing can start up'—
but he too
took his own life. Perhaps he was waiting,
not with that waiting that is itself a
                              transforming energy—
                    'Stone
                    breaks stone to reveal
                    STONE in stone!'—but waiting
to *set all things right,* (to 'rearrange all mysteries
                                        in a new light')
before beginning to live? Not understanding
only conjunctions
                    of song's
                              raging magic
                              with patient courage
                              will make   a new life:
we can't wait: time is
                    not on our side:
                              world
in which those I respect
                              'already live, they're not waiting
for demolition and reconstruction.' No more
'learning as preparation for life.'
                              In my own days and nights
(crawling, it feels like, on hands and knees—leaping
up into the dance!—to fall again, sprawled, stupid—)

189

I'm trying to learn
the other kind of waiting: charge, or recharge, my
                                                batteries.
Get my head together. Mesh. Knit
idiom with idiom in the
'push and shove of events.'
                What I hold fast to
                is what I wrote last May, not Kali speaking:
            'When the pulse rhythms
            of revolution and poetry
            mesh,

            then the singing begins.'
                        But that *when* must be
                        now!
Timid, impatient, halfblinded by
the dazzling abyss, nauseous under
the roar of the avalanche,
'imagination of disaster' a poison
that lurches through me the way
a sickened killer might lurch
through streets of charred straw—

                                —what I hold fast to, grip

in my fist for amulet, is my love
of those who dare, who do dare
to struggle, dare to reject
unlived life, disdain
to die of *that*.

                'Let us become men' says Dan Berrigan.
                'Maybe you see it all, whiteman,
                            or maybe you blind,'
                    says Etheridge Knight to Dan.
                'We gotta work
                at our own pace, slow if need be,
                work together and learn from within,'
                        Richard said to me just today, the day
news of invasion of Laos started to be 'official.'

190

O holy innocents! I have
no virtue but to praise
you who believe
life is possible . . .

FOOTPRINTS (1972)

to J. Laughlin

The Footprints

Someone crossed this field last night:
day reveals
a perspective of lavender caves
across the snow.   Someone
entered the dark woods.

Hut

Mud and wattles.   Round almost.
Moss. Threshold: a writing,
small stones inlaid, footworn.
'Enter, who
so desires.'

Floor, beaten earth.   Walls
shadows.   Ashpit at center.
By day, coming in from
molten green, dusk
profound.   By night, through smokehole,
the star.

A Defeat in the Green Mountains

(Memory of Summer, 1955)

On a dull day she goes
to find the river,
accompanied by two
unwilling children, shut in
among thorns, vines, the
long grass

stumbling, complaining, the
blackflies biting them,
but persists, drawn
by river-sound close beyond
the baffling scratchy thicket

and after a half-hour they emerge
upon the water
                    flowing by
both dark and clear.
          A space and
          a movement crossing
          their halted movement.
But the river is deep

the mud her foot stirs up
frightens her; the kids are
scared and angry. No way
to reach the open fields over there.
Back then:
swamp underfoot, through the

perverse thickets, finding
a path finally to the
main road—defeated,
to ponder the narrow
depth of the river,
its absorbed movement past her.

Yes, I'm nettled.
I touched a leaf
because I like to touch leaves
(even though this one
as it happens, had nothing
of special grace, no shine)

and though it had no spikes,
or thorns attached to it,
nothing like that
to warn the hand,
here I am tingling, it
hurts. I must look

for the coarse, patient
dockleaves nearby,
faithfully awaiting
nettled hands
to soothe with their juice,
wasted otherwise.

Living with a Painting

for Albert Kresch

It ripens
while I sleep, afternoons, on the old sofa,

the forms ready themselves for dazed, refreshed,
wakening senses to bite on,
'taste with the mind's tongue.'

Yes, that confusion
comes of sleep, and all was ripe
before, and I green.
                    Yet it's true
'One who makes it, and one who needs it.'

The work ripens
within the temper of living round about it,
that brings as tribute, as rain,
many awakenings

until a once-cold
arbitrary violet reveals itself
as radiance, a defining halo

and discovered
geometries in interplay

show in their harvest-time
vase, lute, beaker.

1962

198

An Old Friend's Self-Portrait

i

Somber, the mouth pinched and twisted,
eyes half-fierce, half-sad,
the portrait of my old friend stares at me
or at the world; that face
I remember as it laughed
twenty years ago, not untroubled but
more certain, face of an artist who
now with a master's hand paints
the image of his own
in-sight.

ii

Strong, the brow
revealed in volume, the ears
listening,
the eyes
watching time purse the
gentle smiling lips I remember,
this face
writes itself on triple-S board,
signs itself in thick
ridges of paint,
breaks through the mirror.

1970

In love (unless loved) is not *love*.
You're right: x needs—

with azure sparks down dazedly
drifting through vast night
long after—

       the embrace of y to even
begin to become z.
           To x alone
something else happens. Example:

a woman painter returns,
younger than she should be, from travels
in monotone countries

and on arrival, bandages of fatigue
whipped off her eyes,
              instantly
looks, looks at whose shadow
first falls on her primed (primal) canvas
(all the soul she has left
for the moment)—:

At once the light
(not the gray north of journeys)
colors him! Candle-gold,

yet not still, but shivering,
lit white flesh for her (who preferred brown)
and hair light oak or walnut
was mahogany on the dream-palette.

Setting to work, the painter
paints what she sees: the object
moves, her eyes change focus
faithfully, the nimbus
dances.

200

All one year she paints:
the works are known later by titles—
'Fiery Clouds,' 'Alembic,' *'Du Bleu Noir,'* 'The Burning-Glass.'
Rectangles, ovals, all the landscapes are portraits,
x kneels at the feet of y, barbaric frankincense
enclouds her. But y, embarrassed,
and finally indifferent, turns
away. Talking (he is a poet)

talking, walking away, entering
a small boat, the middle distance,

sliding downstream away.
She has before her

a long scroll to paint on, but no room
to follow that river.   The light's going.

'L'homme est un drôle de corps,
qui n'a pas son centre de gravité en lui-même,'
she reads, pages falling from trees
at need around her.   She continues

to paint what she saw:

y is a brushstroke now
in furthest perspective, it hurts

the eyes in dusk to see it, no one,
indeed, will know that speck of fire

but x herself, who has not
(in this example) even begun to become

z, but remains
x, a painter; though not perhaps
unchanged. Older. We'll take

some other symbol to represent
that difference—a or o.

June, 1969

201

After I had cut off my hands
and grown new ones

something my former hands had longed for
came and asked to be rocked.

After my plucked out eyes
had withered, and new ones grown

something my former eyes had wept for
came asking to be pitied.

August, 1969

'White phosphorus, white phosphorus,
mechanical snow,
where are you falling?'

'I am falling impartially on roads and roofs,
on bamboo thickets, on people.
My name recalls rich seas on rainy nights,
each drop that hits the surface eliciting
luminous response from a million algae.
My name is a whisper of sequins. Ha!
Each of them is a disk of fire,
I am the snow that burns.
                    I fall
wherever men send me to fall—
but I prefer flesh, so smooth, so dense:
I decorate it in black, and seek
the bone.'

The theater of war. Offstage
a cast of thousands weeping.

Left center, well-lit, a mound
of unburied bodies,

or parts of bodies. Right,
near some dead bamboo that serves as wings,

a whole body, on which
a splash of napalm is working.

Enter the Bride.

She has one breast, one eye,
half of her scalp is bald.

She hobbles towards center front.
Enter the Bridegroom,

a young soldier, thin, but without
visible wounds. He sees her.

Slowly at first, then faster and faster,
he begins to shudder, to shudder,

to ripple with shudders.   Curtain.

Time to Breathe

*(Adapted from a prose poem
by Jean-Pierre Burgart)*

Evenings enduring, blending
one with the next. Ocean calmly
rocking reflected docks and those
indecipherable roads that
inscribe themselves in sky
way above trajectories of the swifts.

That freshness, over
and over: summer
in folds of your dress, mysterious fabric.
And in the disturbing
gentle grace of your neck.
The same summer shadow
looking out of your eyes.

Night seems to stop short
at the horizon. Perhaps it never
will quite arrive. Perhaps,
renewed in the breath of these
first summer days,
we shall leave off dying.

Hope It's True

Wonder if this very day the Hunza
are leading their charmed lives.
Their limbs anointed with oil of apricot,
are they singing, walking the
high paths? Himalayan
blues you couldn't
cry to, it's
like almond milk, sesame, such goodness,
the blues of joy?

While Nevada whores wake anxious
at airconditioned noon,
figuring a blast some time
may shatter the casinos . . .
While Mississippi babies grunt and die,
tired of hunger
and 'small clashes' rip human guts per
daily usual, closer to Hunza-land than here . . .
While an absurd flag
clatters in dust of lunar winds . . .

is the royal apricot-taster
even now stepping sideways from tree to tree
to check on bitterness?—that no Hunza,
the length of the land, shall eat sorrow?

July, 1969

for John Sinclair

Not to blow the mind but
focus it again, renew its
ferocious innocence, hot-pepper sting of
wonder, impatient love.

Enough energy
to save the world; could be.
'Come Together' winds down,
grimly slow-spiralling,
                           only to recoil
with a snap! We're off!
Some zephyr rising
from choppy seas
        charges itself, lifts to a steady
        sweep, it picks me up, it
picks us up, lift up your heads
O ye gates.

(World's heart
keeps skipping a beat,
sweat crawls on the moon's white
stony face.
            Life's
winding down.) Tighten the spring.
Something is breathing deep. Ozone, oxygen.
Even yet. Kick out the jams.

July 30, 1969

Love Poem

for Mitch

Swimming through dark, slow,
breaststroke—
                    not to startle
                    walls or chairs and
                    wake you—
I almost sundered the
full to the brim with moonlight
mirror

September, 1969

A Place to Live

Honeydew seeds: on impulse
strewn in a pot of earth. Now,

(the green vines) wandering
down over the pot's edges:

certainly no room here to lay
the egg of a big, pale,
green-fleshed melon.
                    Wondering

where the hell to go.

The News

East Boston too, like the fields
somewhere, from which the snow's
    melting to show forth black
    earth and timid
    tips of grass, is preparing
for spring. In the windows
of candy stores are displayed
jump-ropes: white cord and glossy
red-and-green handles.

Obstinate Faith

Branch-lingering oakleaves, dry
brown over gray snowglare,
make of a gust of wind
an instrument, to play
'spring rain.'

Fragment

Not free to love where their liking chooses,
lacking desire for what love proposes,
they wander indoors and out, calling
'Eros, Eros' to the winged one,
who will not listen, for he will bear no bondage . . .

Gary with deer and bear
in the Sierras, in poems.
Acting his dreams out:
kind man,
practical.
Knows
how to kill and skin deer
and how to eat them
and love their life,
love them to life.
Daily his year-old son
runs out to greet them, they browse
deep in his green,
he knows them.

And another Gary
(McDonald) in
New Britain, dreams me
                    a letter to live from—
that day's bread:
'I am just
thinking, writing, breathing here,
phantom of air . . . the
face of the world is
a million eyes.'
Wakes me to know
'there is a way
to the journey. A love grows into itself.'

And a third
(Aspenberg) planning
a Chronicle of the
End of the World, meanwhile
reads my chart: 'Many
loves at first sight.

Visions are presented.
You must choose
the worthy ones to follow.
Your death
may come in a
public place . . .'

'Horoscopes,' he says, 'would make
perfect poems if I could get into them.
Everything relates to all.'

Under a Blue Star

Under a blue star, dragon   of skygate . . .
Such wakenings into twilight, foreboding intermingled
with joy, beyond
hope of knowledge. The days
a web of wires, of energies vibrating
in chords and single
long notes of song; but nights
afloat on dream, dreams
that float silent, or leave word
of blue sky-dragons, to seduce
the day's questions, drown them
in twilight before dawn . . . What gate
opens, dim there in the mind's
field, river-mists of the sky
veiling its guardian?

Sea gulls inland.
Come for a change of diet,
a breath of
earth-air.

I smell the
green, dank, amber, soft
undersides of an old pier in their cries.

3 a.m., September 1, 1969

for Kenneth Rexroth

Warm wind, the leaves
rustling without dryness,
hills dissolved into silver.

It could be any age,
four hundred years ago or a time
of post-revolutionary peace,
the rivers clean again, birth rate and crops
somehow in balance . . .

In heavy dew
under the moon the blond grasses
lean in swathes on the field slope. Fervently
the crickets practice their religion of ectasy.

A New Year's Garland
for My Students/MIT:
1969–70

i   Arthur

In winter, intricately wrapped, the buds
of trees and bushes
are firm and small and go unnoticed,
though their complexity is as beautiful
now as eventual
                 silky leaves in spring.

ii   Barry

What task is it
hidden just beyond vision yet,
your frown tries
to touch, as if
there, almost within
reach of
your eyes' blue light, as if
frowning were weight that
would pin phantoms to the
ground of
knowledge—
                 What Gorgon is it
that shall be given you
(revealed)
                 to strike?

iii   Bill

There is a fence around the garden
but the gate stands open.

And the garden within
is pleasant—
neither drearily formal
nor sad with neglect:

oldfashioned, with shade-trees and places
to take the sun, with paths
planted with fragrant resilient herbs.

But looking
out of the thickest, darkest branches—
back of the stone pool,
behind the arbor—

eyes of some animal:

blue-green gray, are they?
Topaz?
         They question
and propose

no answers yet; disquieting
in the still garden,
and disquieted.

iv   Don

If the body is a house,
the house a temple,

in that temple
is a labyrinth,

in that labyrinth's core
a vast room,

in the room's remote depths
an altar,

upon the altar
a battle raging, raging,

between two angels, one feathered
with spines, with sharp flames,

one luminous, the subtle
angel of understanding,

and from time to time a smile flickers
on the face of the mean angel

and slips, shadowy, over
to the gentle face.

v   **Ernie**

Hey Ernie, here you come suavely
round the corner in your
broken-windowed bus
and brake elegantly and swing
open the door so I can get in and ride on, sitting
on crumpled poems among guitars and
percussion sets.
What can I say, Ernie?—
Younger than my son, you are
nevertheless my old friend

whom I trust.

vi   Judy

You have the light step
of Ariel, the smile of Puck,
something of Rosalind's
courage, I think, though you are small
as I imagine Perdita to have been

(and why Shakespeare gets into all this at all
I don't know—but he does, insistently)

but when you set off alone, winter nights,
coat collar up, and in your pocket
that invisible flute,

it's myself I think of, 12 years old,
trudging home from the library lugging
too many books, and seeing

visions in Ilford High Road,

the passing faces oblivious
to all their own strange beauty under the street-lamps,

and I drunk on it.

vii   Lucy

Lucy taking
the family cat
along on her pilgrimage.

Lucy's nineteenth-century face
gazing steadfastly into the twenty first century.

Jewish Lucy
rooted in Emily's
New England fields.

Aquarian Lucy searching
for rhymes that dance,

for gestures that speak of
the rhyming seasons,

for the community
of poems and people.

viii   Margo

The one who can't say it
says it.

The one who can't figure how
pictures what.

The song no one can sing
sounds, quiet
air in air.

ix   Mark

Ripple of clear water
in the sun—inscape of moving, curling wavelets,
and the murmuring of them: an ideogram
for 'happiness'—

a buddha spring upwelling
in deep woods
where light must climb
down ladders of somber
needled branches.

i

The old poet, white-bearded
showing an antique motorcycle
to the children of the revolution.

The old poet overhearing
lovers telling one another poems,
and the poems are his.
His laugh rings out in sudden joy
as it did when he was twenty-one.
I hunger for a world
you can
live in forever.

ii

'The very essence
of destiny hung over this house'
(this time) *'and how was he,*
a membrane stretched between the
light and darkness of the world,
not to become conscious of it?'

I want
a world you can live in.

'The blood ran to his head
and his heart beat like a trip-hammer
when he thought of
encountering the man,
of finding himself in his presence.

It was not cowardice; it was only that he had become
shudderingly aware of the tremendous task he
                              had undertaken
and when he had realized it completely,
to the very tips of his fingers and the depths of
                              his soul,

217

he smiled,
feeling rather like a man standing on the roof of
                                        a burning house,
and marking
the spot on which he must without fail alight. . .
He must indeed be
a good jumper,
and something of a magician besides.'

I want
a world.

xi   Roger

'Mad prince'—OK—that's it—
a madness
of such simplicity
                under the crown of
                too much knowledge
                        (heavy on your head its
                        velvet and stupidly
                        glaring stones, as
                        on all our heads
                        that burden, all of us
                        weighed down with its despair)
that it lifts
out and through it

like your Jewish natural would escape
a rabbi's hat, and send it sailing
crazy into the sky
of pale funny blue like your eyes.

xii   Ted

The people in you:
some are silent.

Two I see clear:

a girl at the edge of the sea
who dances in solitude
for joy at the sea's dance;
and she is one who speaks.

And an old man nearby
in a dark hut, who sits looking
into a pit of terror: hears
horror creeping upon the sea.
And he is silent.

Her voice lifts, silvery,
a flying shower in the sunlight

but the sky darkens, sea-music
twists into hideous tumult.
Other shadowy figures

move on the shore of my dream of you:
their lips form words but no sound
comes forth. None can speak

until the old man raises
his grim head and shouts
his curse or warning.

xiii   Vic

The dog, Stalin, is free and foolish
as a holy hasid.
Wonder, arf, wonder wags his tail,
in him your soul
takes its rest and,
          twitching, sighing,
          lifting sensitive ears at odd noises,
grows.

To Kevin O'Leary, Wherever He Is

Dear elusive Prince of Ireland,
I have received
from Arizona
your letter, with no return address
                              but telling me
my name in Hebrew, and its meaning:
    entrance, exit,
    way through of
    giving and receiving,
    which are one.
Hallelujah! It's as if you'd sent me
in the U.S. mails
a well of water,
    a frog at its brim, and mosses;
sent me a cold and sweet freshness
dark to taste.
            Love from the door,
            Daleth.

The Day the Audience Walked Out on Me, and Why

(May 8th, 1970, Goucher College, Maryland)

Like this it happened:
after the antiphonal reading from the psalms
and the dance of lamentation before the altar,
and the two poems, 'Life at War' and
                  'What Were They Like?'
I began my rap,
and said:

Yes, it is well that we have gathered
in this chapel to remember
the students shot at Kent State,

but let us be sure we know
our gathering is a mockery unless
we remember also
the black students shot at Orangeburg two years ago,
and Fred Hampton murdered in his bed
by the police only months ago.

And while I spoke the people
—girls, older women, a few men—
began to rise and turn
their backs to the altar and leave.

And I went on and said,
Yes, it is well that we remember
all of these, but let us be sure
we know it is hypocrisy
to think of them unless
we make our actions their memorial,
actions of militant resistance.

By then the pews were almost empty
and I returned to my seat and a man stood up
in the back of the quiet chapel
(near the wide-open doors through which
the green of May showed, and the long shadows
                         of late afternoon)
and said my words
desecrated a holy place.

And a few days later
when some more students (black) were shot
at Jackson, Mississippi,
no one desecrated the white folks' chapel,
because no memorial service was held.

Pig and wasp are robbed of their names.
OK! Let brutal
Amerikan polizei
and tightassed DAR's be known forever
as pigs and wasps, but let's think up
new names for those we ripped off:

the roguish Black Berkshires, the intelligent
rangy ginger roamers of Mexican beaches,
Iowan acorn-eaters, fast on their small feet,
even the oppressed pink fatbacks in smelly
concentration-pens,
                    deserve a good name.

And the bees' ornery cousins—
oh, in the time of ripened pears,
of plum and fig burst open for very languor
of sweetness and juicy weight—
then you shall see the spiteful, buzzing, honeyless ones
graceful with ecstasy, clumsy with passion,
humble in pleasure no pale wasp
knows. What
shall their new name be?

Leather Jacket

She turns, eager—
hand going out to touch
his arm. But touches
a cold thick sleeve.

1970

He told me about
a poem he was writing.
For me.

He told me it asked,
'When I mean only to brush her gently
with soft feathers,

do the feathers
turn into needles?'
His telling me

was a cloud of
soft feathers, I closed
my eyes and sank in it.

Many weeks
I waited. At last,
'Did you, were you able

to finish that poem
you told me about,
once?'

'No,' he said,
looking away.
Needles paused

for an instant on my skin
before they drew blood.

1970

For weeks the poem of your body,
of my hands upon your body
    stroking, sweeping, in the rite of
    worship, going
    their way of wonder down
    from neck-pulse to breast-hair to level
    belly to cock—
for weeks that poem, that prayer,
unwritten.
        The poem unwritten, the act
left in the mind, undone. The years
a forest of giant stones, of fossil stumps,
blocking the altar.

1970

The Good Dream

Rejoicing
because we had met again
we rolled laughing
over and over upon the big bed.

The joy was
not in a narrow sense
erotic—not
narrow in any sense.
It was

that all impediments,
every barrier, of history,
of learn'd anxiety,
wrong place and wrong time,

had gone down,
vanished.
It was the joy

of two rivers
meeting in depths of the sea.

1970

Goethe's Blues

(Fantasia on the
Trilogie der Leidenschaft)

i

The hills stirring under their woven
leaf-nets, sighing, shimmering. . .
High summer.
                    And he with
April anguish tearing him,
heart a young animal, its fur
curly and legs too long.

But he is old. Sere.

> 'O love, O love,
> not unkind,
> kind,
>
> my life goes out of me
> breath by breath
>
> thinking of your austere
> compassion.'

ii

Fame tastes 'sweet' to him,
too sweet, and then sour,
and then not at all.

It is not a substance
to taste, it is a box
in which he is kept.

226

He is a silver
dandelion seed entrapped
in a cube of plexiglass.

iii

'Stop the coach! I want to get out
and die!'
      His friends
wonder what he's scribbling,
'furiously,' as it is said,
all the way back.
They're doing 80, the freeway's
all theirs.
      'Nature smiles,
and smiles, and
says nothing. And I'm
driving away from the gates of
Paradise.'

1970

The trees' black hair electric
brushed out,
        fierce haloes.

And westward
veils of geranium hold their own,
even yet. Transparent.

People are quickly, buoyantly
crossing the Common
into evening, into
a world of promises.

It was the custom of my tribe
to speak and sing;
not only to share the present, breath and sight,
but to the unborn.
Still, even now, we reach out
toward survivors. It is a covenant
of desire.

        Shall there be, by long chance,
one to hear me after the great, the gross,
              the obscene silence,
to hear and wonder that in the last days
the seasons gave joy,
that dusk transmuted
        brilliant pink to lilac, lilac
        to smoke blue?

And lovers sat on a bench in the cold as night drew in,
laughing because the snow had melted.

The Sun Going Down upon Our Wrath

You who are so beautiful—
your deep and childish faces,
your tall bodies—

Shall I warn you?

Do you know
what it was to have
a certitude of grasses waving
upon the earth though all
humankind were dust?
Of dust returning
to fruitful dust?

Do you already know
what hope is fading from us
and pay no heed,
see the detested grave-worm shrivel,
the once-despised,
and not need it?

Is there an odyssey
your feet pull you towards
away from now to walk
the waters, the fallen
orchard stars?
                    It seems
your fears are only the old fears, antique
anxieties, how graceful;
they lay as cloaks on shoulders
of men long dead,
skirts of sorrow wrapped
over the thighs of legendary women.

Can you be warned?

If you are warned will your beauty
scale off, to leave
gaping meat livid with revulsion?

No, who can believe it.
Even I in whose heart
stones rattle, rise each day
to work and imagine.

Get wisdom, get understanding, saith
the ancient. But he believed
there is nothing new under the sun,
his future
rolled away in great coils forever
into the generations.
Among conies the grass
grew again
and among bones.
And the bones would rise.

If there is time to warn you,
if you believed there shall be
never again a green blade in the crevice,
luminous eyes in rockshadow:
if you were warned and believed
the warning,

would your beauty
break into spears of fire,

fire to turn fire, a wall
of refusal, could there be
a reversal I cannot

hoist myself high enough
to see,
plunge myself deep enough
to know?

Forest Altar, September

The gleam of thy drenched
floors of leaf-layers! Fragrance
of death and change!
                    If there is only
now to live, I'll live
the hour till doomstroke
crouched with the russet toad,
my huge human size
no more account than a bough fallen:

not upward,
searching for branch-hidden sky:
I'll look
down into paradise.

Thy moss gardens, the deep
constellations of green, the striate
rock furred with emerald,
inscribed with gold lichen,
with scarlet!
                    Thy smooth
acorns in roughsurfaced
precise cups!
                    Thy black
horns of plenty!

Joie de Vivre

All that once hurt
(healed) goes on hurting
in new ways. One same heart
—not a transplant—
cut down to the stump
throbs, new, old.
Bring paper and pencil
out of the dimlit into
the brightlit room, make sure
all you say is true.
'Antonio, Antonio,
the old wound's
bleeding.' 'Let it bleed.'
The pulse of life-pain
strong again, count it,
fast but
not fluttering.

The Wanderer

The chameleon who wistfully
thought it could not suffer
nostalgia

now on a vast sheet of clear glass
cowers, and prays for vision
of russet bark and trembling foliage.

i

The old wooden house a soft
almost-blue faded green
embowered in southern autumn's
nearly-yellow green leaves,
the air damp after a night of rain.

ii

The black girl sitting alone in the back row
smiled at me.

iii

Yes, in strange kitchens
I know where to find the forks,

and among another woman's perfume bottles
I can find the one that suits me,

and in the bedrooms
of children I have not met
I have galloped the island
of Chincoteague at 3 a.m., too tired to sleep—

but beyond that

at how many windows I have listened
to the cricket-quivering of borrowed moonlight.

iv

Brass tacks that glint
                    illumination of dailiness
              and hold down feet to earth
                          ears to the rush and whisper of
                                the ring and rattle of
                                    the Great Chain—
brass tacks that rivet
the eyes to Consolation,
              that *are* Consolation.

v

Weighed down by two shopping bags she trudges
uphill diagonally across the nameless (but grassy)
East Boston square—Fort Something,
it was once. Her arms ache, she wonders
if some items she is carrying deserve to be classed
as conspicuous consumption. It would be nice
if a gray pet donkey came by magic
to meet her now, panniers ready
for her burdens. . . She looks up,
and the weight
lifts: behind the outstretched eager
bare limbs and swaying twigs of two
still-living elms

in moonstone blue of dusk
the new moon itself is swinging
back and forth on a cloud-trapeze!

vi

The spring snow
is flying
          aslant
                over the crocus gold
                and into evening.

vii

Returning tired towards his temporary
lodging, wondering again
if his workday was useful at all

the human being saw the rose-colored leaves
of a small plant growing among
the stones of a low wall

unobtrusively, and found himself
standing quite still, gazing,
and found himself
smiling.

The Old King

for Jim Forest

The Soul's dark Cottage, batter'd and decay'd,
Lets in new Light through chinks that Time hath made.

And at night—
the whole night a cavern, the world
an abyss—

lit from within:

a red glow
throbbing at the chinks.

Far-off a wanderer
unhoused, unhouseled,
wonders to see
hearthblaze:
fears, and takes heart.

The world comes back to me
eager and hungry, and often
too tired to wag its tail,

a dog with wanderlust
back from South Boston or the Reservoir.

Keeps coming back,
brought by triumphant strangers
who don't understand he knows the way well.
Faint jingle of collartag breaking
my sleep, he arrives
and patiently scratches himself on the front steps.
I let in blue
daybreak,
in rushes the world,

visible dog concocted
of phantasmagoric atoms.
Nudges my hand with wet nose,
flumps down, deeply sighing,

smelling of muddy streams, of thrown-away treasures,
of some exotic news, not blood, not flowers,
and not his own fur—
                  unable
except by olifact
to tell me anything.
                Where have I been
without the world? Why am I glad
he wolfs his food and gathers
strength for the next journey?

crossing furrows from green hedge to hedge,
rather a crawling out of one's deep hole

in midfield, in the moist
gray that is dawn, and begins

to hurt the eyes;
                        to sit on one's haunches
gazing, listening, picking up
the voices of wheat, trail of other
animals telling the nose the night's news.

To be at the hollow center of a field
at dawn; the radius
radiant. Silver
to gold, shadows
violet dancers.

                        By noon the builders
scream in, the horizon
blocks afternoon, a jagged
restlessness. To be
an animal dodging
pursuers it smells but can't
see clear, through labyrinths

of new walls. To be mangled or
grow wise in escape.
To bite, and destroy the net.

                        To make it maybe
into the last of day, and witness
crimson wings
                        cutting down after
the sun gone down in wrath.

237

To stay perhaps,

> one throat far-off
> pulsing to venture
> one note from its feathers,
> one bell,

on into dewfall, into
peculiar silence.

The multitude gone, labyrinths
crumbling.
> To go down
back into the known hole.

Alice Transfixed

When your huge face
whipped by the highest branches
finds itself peering into a nest,
pathos of scraggly twigs and tiny eggs:

and the appalled mother-bird is shrieking
'Serpent! Serpent!' at you,
her beak grazing your ear—

that's when you wonder
if the first wish, the first question,
were worth it.
Mournfully
the feet you have bade-farewell-to
trample in cloudhidden thickets,
crushing the slow beasts.

Memories of John Keats

for Mitch

Watchfulness and sensation as John Keats
said to me
for it was to me
he said it
            (and to you)

Side by side we lay full-length
upon a spumy rock, envisioning
Ailsa Craig

                    The sea tumult
bore away
            a word
      and a word

And again *that which is creative
must create itself*   he said
We skirted
the murmurous green hollow
Vale of Health

strolling the spiral road, the
Vale of Soulmaking

He would stop to pluck
a leaf, finger
a stone

watchfulness was his word
sensation
            *and watchfulness in itself
the Genius
of Poetry must work out
its own salvation in a man*

I leapt   he said
headlong into the sea. . .

239

Blue of Ireland quickens in the sea,
green fish
        deep below the fathoms
of glass air.

My shadow
if I were floating free

would stroke the mountains' bristles
pensively, a finger of dark

smaller even than the plane's
tiny shadow, unnoticed,

nearing the edge of
        the old world.

By Rail through the Earthly Paradise, Perhaps Bedfordshire

The fishermen among the fireweed.

Towpath and humpbacked bridge. Cows
in one field, slabs of hay
ranged in another.

Common day
precious to me.
There's nothing else
to grasp.

The train
moves me past it too fast, not much,
just a little, I don't want
to stay for ever.
                    Horses,
three of them, flowing across a paddock
as wind flows over barley.

Oaks in parkland, distinct,
growing their shadows.
A man from Cairo across from me
reading *A Synopsis of Eye Physiology.*
The brickworks,
fantastical slender chimneys.

I'm not hungry,
not lonely. It seems
at times I want nothing,
no human giving and taking.
Nothing I see
fails to give pleasure,

no thirst for righteousness
dries my throat, I am silent
and happy, and troubled only
by my own happiness. Looking,

looking and naming. I wish the train now
would halt for me at a station in the fields,
(the name goes by
unread).
            In the deep aftermath
of its faded rhythm, I could become

a carved stone
set in the gates of the earthly paradise,

an angler's fly
lost in the sedge to watch the centuries.

The Cabbage Field

Both Taine and the inland English child
were mocked for their independent
comparison of the sea to a field of cabbages:

but does this field
of blue and green and purple curling
turmoil of ordered curves, reaching

out to the smoky twilight's immense
ambiguousness we call
horizon, resemble

anything but the sea?

In Silence

Clear from the terraced mountainside
through fretwork of laden vines, red apples, brown
heavy pears poised to fall, and not falling,
I saw a woman deep in the valley
wrapped in a blue cloak as if autumn
veiled in the ripe sun
were running its cutting-edge over her skin,
hurry from her house out to the garden swimming pool
and bend to greet a child there, and again hurry
round the pool to the far side,
and drop the cloak from her shoulders,
kick off her shoes in haste
and at last slowly, smoothly,
flowingly as if all her being
were blue water,
enter the blue water.

Brunnenburg, 1971

To Antonio Machado

Here in the mountain woods
a furious small fountain
is channelled through pipes of hollow sapling
into a great wooden vat bevelled with moss,
and thence brims over into a concrete cistern
and from the cistern quietly
in modest rills
into the meadow where cows graze
and fringed wild carnations, white and sweet,
grow by the path.
Machado,
   old man,
      dead man,
   I wish you were here alive
to drink of the cold, earthtasting, faithful spring,
to receive the many voices
of this one brook,
to see its dances
of fury and gentleness,
to write the austere poem
you would have known in it.

Brunnenburg, 1971

Sun, Moon, and Stones

'I longed to go away, to take to the desolate,
denuded mountains opposite me and walk and
walk, without seeing anything but sun, moon,
and stones.'

—*Nikos Kazantzakis*

Sun
moon
stones

>   but where shall we find
>   water?

Sun

>   hoists all things upward and outward
>   thrusts
>   a sword of thirst into the mouth.

Moon

>   fills the womb with ice.

Stones: weapons that carry
>   warmth into night
>   dew into day, and break
>   the flesh of stumbling feet.

And we were born to that sole end:
>   to thirst and grow
>   to shudder
>   to dream in lingering dew, lingering warmth
>   to stumble searching.

But O the fountains,
>   where shall we find them.

Man Alone

When the sun goes down, it writes
a secret name in its own blood for remembrance,
the excess of light
an ardor slow to cool:
and man has time to seek shelter.

But when the moon
gains the horizon, though it tarries
a moment, it vanishes
without trace of silver

and he is left with the stars only,
fierce and remote, and not revealing
the stones of the dark roads.

So it is with the gods,
and with the halfgods,
and with the heroes.

Road

The wayside bushes waiting, waiting.
There's no one,
no one to meet them.
Golden in my sunset dustcloud
I too pass by.

A glimpsed world, halfway through the film,
one slow shot of a ward at night

holds me when the rest is quickly
losing illusion. Strange hold,

as of romance, of glamor: not because
even when I lived in it I had

illusions about that world: simply because
I did live there and it was

a world. Greenshaded lamp glowing
on the charge desk, clipboards
stacked on the desk for the night,

sighs and waiting, waiting-for-morning stirrings
in the dim long room, warm, orderly,
and full of breathings as a cowbarn.

Death and pain dominate this world, for though
many are cured, they leave still weak,

still tremulous, still knowing mortality
has whispered to them; have seen in the folding
of white bedspreads according to rule

the starched pleats of a shroud.
                                    It's against that frozen
counterpane, and the knowledge too
how black an old mouth gaping at death can look

that the night routine has in itself—
without illusions—glamor, perhaps. It had

a rhythm, a choreographic decorum:
when all the evening chores had been done

and a multiple restless quiet listened
to the wall-clock's pulse, and turn by turn

the two of us made our rounds
on tiptoe, bed to bed,

counting by flashlight how many pairs
of open eyes were turned to us,

noting all we were trained to note,
we were gravely dancing—starched

in our caps, our trained replies,
our whispering aprons—the well-rehearsed

pavanne of power. Yes, wasn't it power,
and not compassion,
                                        gave our young hearts
their hard fervor? I hated

to scrub out lockers, to hand out trays of
unappetizing food, and by day, or the tail-end of night

(daybreak dull on gray faces—ours and theirs)
the anxious hurry, the scolding old-maid bosses.
But I loved the power
of our ordered nights,

       gleaming surfaces I'd helped to polish
making patterns in the shipshape
halfdark—
       loved
the knowing what to do, and doing it,
list of tasks getting shorter

hour by hour. And knowing
all the while that Emergency
might ring with a case to admit, anytime,

if a bed were empty. Poised,
ready for that.
       The camera
never returned to the hospital ward,

the story moved on into the streets,
into the rooms where people lived.

But I got lost in the death rooms a while,
remembering being (crudely, cruelly,

just as a soldier or one of the guards
from Dachau might be) in love with order,

an angel like the *chercheuses de poux*, floating
noiseless from bed to bed,

smoothing pillows, tipping
water to parched lips, writing

details of agony carefully into the Night Report.

At the 'Mass Ave Poetry Hawkers' Reading
in the Red Book Cellar

When even craning my neck
I couldn't see over and round
to where poems were sounding from

I found eyesight wasn't so utterly
my way of being
as I'd supposed: each voice

was known to me, I could name
each, and conjure seven
faces, seven heads of

mysteriously intense and living
hair, curly, wavy, straight, dark, light,
or going further, *not* conjure

any picture: solely hear
person in voice: further:
to listen deeper:

deep listening: into the earth
burrowing, into the water courses
hidden in rockbed.

And songs from these
beloved strangers, these close friends,
moved in my blind illumined head,
songs of terror, of hopes unknown to me,
terror, dread: songs of knowledge, songs
of their lives wandering

out into oceans.

1972

Richard's lover has the look,
robust and pure, of a nineteenth-century
Russian heroine. Surely her brows and chin,
smooth hair, free walk,
            and the way she can sit poised and quiet,
speak of depth.

           Across the room
his profile—all I can see
beyond the range of heads and shoulders,
in smoke, in candlelight—
looks off into inner distance,
poignant, a little
           older than last year,
still very young though.

I think she is watching him too.

Calmly, calmly, I am seeing them both.
Reassured.

1972

The Life around Us

for David Mitchell and David Hass

Poplar and oak awake
all night. And through
all weathers of the days of the year.
There is a consciousness
undefined.
Yesterday's twilight, August
almost over, lasted, slowly changing,
until daybreak. Human sounds
were shut behind curtains.
No human saw the night in this garden,
sliding blue into morning.
Only the sightless trees,
without braincells, lived it
and wholly knew it.

Knowing the Way

The wood-dove utters
slowly
      those words he has
to utter,
and softly.
      But takes flight
boldly,
and flies fast.

To Stay Alive

Some people mentioned in these poems, Dennis Riordon, Chuck Matthei, Bob Gilliam, David Worstell, de Courcy Squire and Jennie Orvino were young active war-resisters. 'Robert' referred to the poet Robert Duncan, 'Bromige' to the poet David Bromige. Mitch was my husband Mitch Goodman; the trial referred to in 'Prologue: An Interim' was the one in which he, Dr. Benjamin Spock and three others were defendants. Richard, Boat and Neil were young members of revolutionary collectives. Other personal names refer to various friends, living and dead.

PAGE

118 The quoted lines—'a clearing/in the selva oscura, . . .'—are an adaptation of some lines in 'Selva Oscura' by the late Louis Mac-Neice, a poem much loved by my sister, Olga.

137 *Life that/wants to live.* Albert Schweitzer's phrase, in formulating the basis of his sense of 'reverence for life': 'I am life that wants to live, among other forms of life that want to live.'

137 (*Unlived life/of which one can die.*) Rilke's phrase from *The Notebook of Malte Laurids Brigge.*

141 'Goldengrove/is unleaving all around me'—refers to Gerard Manley Hopkins's 'Spring and Fall: To a Young Child.'

152 *Thursday, May 15th*—the day in 1969 when James Rector was killed, Alan Blanchard, an artist, blinded, and many people wounded by police buckshot fire while protesting the destruction of the People's Park.

154 WHAT PEOPLE CAN DO—from an issue of *The Instant News*, a daily information sheet published in Berkeley during the weeks of demonstrations.

158 *'Keiner/oder Alle, Alles/oder Nichts!'* The lines from Brecht are a refrain of a song about slaves casting off their chains: 'No one or everyone, all or nothing!'

163 'Casa Felice'—the house of friends on Cape Cod.

165 'I Thirst'—Words of Jesus from the Cross, according to John 19:28. The demonstration of May 9, 1970, attempted to make clear the relationship between war abroad and racism and political oppression at home.

172 Powell—the British right-wing politician Enoch Powell.

172 Tube—the London subway system.

173 'Imagination of disaster . . . life/ferocious and sinister'—Henry James, in a letter to Henry Adams.

175 José Yglesias—the quotation is from *In the Fist of the Revolution* (Vintage Books, New York, 1969, p. 89).

186 'By the post house . . . *Wild Mulberry Branch.*' 'Now snow-storms . . . travelling-clothes.' From a translation by David Lattimore of Mao Chi'i-ling, 'To the Air: Southern Branch (At an inn west of the Huai I receive a letter from Ch'en Ching-chih. Sent with a reply.)' See the *Brown University Alumni Monthly,* December, 1969.

188 Kali—the Hindu goddess of rage; the Black Mother.

189 Mayakovsky—the Russian poet Vladimir Mayakovsky (1893–1930). The quotation is from his *How Are Verses Made?* (G. M. Hyde, tr., Grossman, 1970). Though William Carlos Williams did not read Russian, he did *see* Mayakovsky's poems; and though his own structural inventions came out of rhythmic, sonic, expressive necessities of his own, I surmise the visual impression of Mayakovsky's lines may have remained with him as a hint. See his 'Russia,' first published in *The Clouds* (1948), and included in *The Collected Later Poems* (New Directions, 1963).

189 'Stone/breaks stone. . . .' From an inscription on an ancient Chinese painting, 'Hamlet Between Cliffs,' by Tao Chi.

190 'Let us become men'—adapted from what Father Berrigan said in his last 'underground' speech, before his recapture in 1970, at a rally in support of the people who had destroyed draft files by immersing them in chemicals manufactured by the Du Pont Corporation. He said, in part: 'Let us therefore trust what we have done. Let us multiply the same and similar acts. Let us trust one another. Let us draw near across great differences, exorcize together our fear. Let us do that one thing . . . which by common and cowardly agreement is forbidden in America to-day—let us be men.'

190 Etheridge Knight—the poet, editor and part author of *Black Voices from Prison*. The quotation is from 'To Dan Berrigan,' in the November, 1970, issue of *Motive*, of which Knight was poetry editor; the magazine also carried the text of Father Berrigan's speech, cited above.

Footprints

About two thirds of the poems in this volume were written concurrently with the 'notebook' poem that gave its name to *To Stay Alive*. The rest were written—some in England during the summer of

1971—subsequently, except for a few which got 'lost' during the compilation of earlier volumes.

195   'Hut'—This poem is a pendant to the poem 'Relearning the Alphabet.'

201   *'L'homme est . . ./en lui-même'*—'Humans are strange creatures, whose center of gravity lies outside their own body.' These words are by the French poet Francis Ponge (1899–).

204   'Time to Breathe'—adapted from an untitled prose poem in *Ombres,* by Jean-Pierre Burgart (Mercure de France, Paris, 1965).

205   'Hunza'—residents of a small mountain kingdom in northwest Kashmir, noted for their health and longevity.

206   'M. C. 5'—the rock group associated with the White Panthers in Motor City. John Sinclair: poet, revolutionary, sometime political prisoner. The poem was written while listening to the record album *Kick Out the Jams* during the moon-landings.

217   *'Richard* (ii)'—the quoted lines are adapted from *The Maurizius Case,* by Jakob Wasserman (1928).

232   'Antonio, Antonio,/the old wound's/bleeding.'—a quote from 'Cranach,' in Sir Herbert Read's *Collected Poems* (Faber and Faber, London, 1946; New Directions, New York, 1951).

235   The italicized lines are from Edmund Waller (1606–87).

237   'Life Is Not a Walk across a Field'—Boris Pasternak, from a Russian proverb.

238   'Alice Transfixed'—see Chapter V of Lewis Carroll's *Alice in Wonderland.*

239   The italicized words are all quotes from John Keats's letters, as in the phrase 'the Vale of Soulmaking.' The 'Vale of Health' is a part of Hampstead Heath, London, near which the poet lived.

242   'Both Taine and the inland English child'—H. A. Taine was the French literary historian (1828–93), while the 'English child' is mentioned in an essay by G. K. Chesterton.

243   Antonio Machado—Spanish poet (1875–1939).

248   *'chercheuses de poux'*—a reference to the poem 'The Women Hunting Lice' by Arthur Rimbaud (1854–91). The prose translation by Anthony Hartley in *The Penguin Book of French Verse,* Volume III, begins: 'When the child's brow full of red torments begs for the white swarm of lazy dreams, tall charming sisters with delicate fingers and silvery nails come near his bed.'

INDEX OF TITLES

New Directions Paperbooks—A Partial Listing

Walter Abish, *How German Is It.* NDP508.
Ahmed Ali, *Twilight in Delhi.* NDP782.
John Allman, *Scenarios for a Mixed Landscape.*
  NDP619.
Alfred Andersch, *Efraim's Book.* NDP779.
Sherwood Anderson, *Poor White.* NDP763.
Wayne Andrews, *The Surrealist Parade.* NDP689.
David Antin, *Tuning.* NDP570.
G. Apollinaire, *Selected Writings.*† NDP310.
Jimmy S. Baca, *Martín & Meditations.* NDP648.
Balzac, *Colonel Chabert.* NDP848.
Djuna Barnes, *Nightwood.* NDP98.
J. Barzun, *An Essay on French Verse.* NDP708.
H. E. Bates, *A Month by the Lake.* NDP669.
  A Party for the Girls. NDP653.
Charles Baudelaire, *Flowers of Evil.* †NDP684.
  Paris Spleen. NDP294.
Bei Dao, *Old Snow.* NDP727.
Gottfried Benn, *Primal Vision.* NDP322.
Adolfo Bioy Casares, *A Russian Doll.* NDP745.
Carmel Bird, *The Bluebird Café.* NDP707.
Johannes Bobrowski, *Shadow Lands.* NDP788.
Wolfgang Borchert, *The Man Outside.* NDP319.
Jorge Luis Borges, *Labyrinths.* NDP186.
  Seven Nights. NDP576.
Kay Boyle, *The Crazy Hunter.* NDP770.
  Fifty Stories. NDP741.
Kamau Brathwaite, *MiddlePassages.* NDP776.
  Black + Blues. NDP815.
William Bronk, *Selected Poems.* NDP816.
M. Bulgakov, *Flight & Bliss.* NDP593.
  The Life of M. de Moliere. NDP601.
Frederick Busch, *Absent Friends.* NDP721.
Veza Canetti, *Yellow Street.* NDP709.
Anne Carson, *Glass, Irony & God.* NDP808.
Joyce Cary, *Mister Johnson.* NDP631.
Hayden Carruth, *Tell Me Again. . . .* NDP677.
Camilo José Cela, *Mazurka for Two Dead Men.*
  NDP789.
Louis-Ferdinand Céline,
  Death on the Installment Plan. NDP330.
  Journey to the End of the Night. †NDP542.
René Char, *Selected Poems.* †NDP734.
Jean Cocteau, *The Holy Terrors.* NDP212.
M. Collis, *She Was a Queen.* NDP716.
Gregory Corso, *Long Live Man.* NDP127.
  Herald of the Autochthonic Spirit. NDP522.
Robert Creeley, *Windows.* NDP687.
Guy Davenport, *7 Greeks.* NDP799.
Margaret Dawe, *Nissequott.* NDP775.
Osamu Dazai, *The Setting Sun.* NDP258.
  No Longer Human. NDP357.
Mme. de Lafayette, *The Princess of Cleves.*
  NDP660.
Debra DiBlasi, *Drought.* NDP836.
Robert Duncan, *Selected Poems.* NDP754.
Wm. Empson, *7 Types of Ambiguity.* NDP204.
S. Endo, *Deep River.* NDP820.
  The Samurai. NDP839.
Caradoc Evans, *Nothing to Pay.* NDP800.
Wm. Everson, *The Residual Years.* NDP263.
Lawrence Ferlinghetti, *A Coney Island of the Mind.*
  NDP74.
  These Are My Rivers. NDP786.
Ronald Firbank, *Five Novels.* NDP581.
F. Scott Fitzgerald, *The Crack-up.* NDP757.
Gustave Flaubert, *A Simple Heart.* NDP819.
J. Gahagan, *Did Gustav Mahler Ski?* NDP711.
Forrest Gander, *Science & Steepleflower.* NDP861.
Gandhi, *Gandi on Non-Violence.* NDP197.
Gary, Romain, *Promise at Dawn.* NDP635.
W. Gerhardie, *Futility.* NDP722.
Goethe, *Faust,* Part I. NDP70.
Allen Grossman, *Philosopher's Window.* NDP807.
Martin Grzimek, *Shadowlife.* NDP705.
Guigonnat, Henri, *Daemon in Lithuania.* NDP592.
Lars Gustafsson, *The Death of a Beekeeper.* NDP523.
  A Tiler's Afternoon. NDP761.
Knut Hamsun, *Dreamers.* NDP821.

John Hawkes, *The Beetle Leg.* NDP239.
  Second Skin. NDP146.
H. D. *Collected Poems.* NDP611.
  Helen in Egypt. NDP380.
  Selected Poems. NDP658.
  Tribute to Freud. NDP572.
  Trilogy. NDP866.
Herman Hesse, *Siddhartha.* NDP65.
Susan Howe, *The Nonconformist's Memorial.*
  NDP755.
Vicente Huidobro, *Selected Poetry.* NDP520.
C. Isherwood, *All the Conspirators.* NDP480.
  The Berlin Stories. NDP134.
Lêdo Ivo, *Snake's Nest.* NDP521.
Fleur Jaeggy, *Last Vanities.* NDP856.
Henry James, *The Sacred Fount.* NDP790.
Gustav Janouch, *Conversations with Kafka.* NDP313.
Alfred Jarry, *Ubu Roi.* NDP105.
Robinson Jeffers, *Cawdor and Medea.* NDP293.
B. S. Johnson, *Christie Malry's. . .* NDP600.
G. Josipovici, *In a Hotel Garden.* NDP801.
James Joyce, *Stephen Hero.* NDP133.
Franz Kafka, *Amerika.* NDP117.
Mary Karr, *The Devil's Tour.* NDP768.
Bob Kaufman, *The Ancient Rain.* NDP514.
John Keene, *Annotations.* NDP809.
H. von Kleist, *Prince Friedrich.* NDP462.
Dezsö Kosztolányi, *Anna Edes.* NDP772.
Rüdiger Kremer, *The Color of Snow.* NDP743.
M. Krleža, *On the Edge of Reason.* NDP810.
Jules Laforgue, *Moral Tales.* NDP594.
P. Lal, *Great Sanskrit Plays.* NDP142.
Tommaso Landolfi, *Gogol's Wife.* NDP155.
D. Larsen, *Stitching Porcelain.* NDP710.
James Laughlin, *The Secret Room.* NDP837.
Lautréamont, *Maldoror.* NDP207.
D. H. Lawrence, *Quetzalcoatl.* NDP864.
Siegfried Lenz, *The German Lesson.* NDP618.
Denise Levertov, *Breathing the Water.* NDP640.
  Collected Earlier Poems 1940–60. NDP475.
  The Life Around Us. NDP843.
  Poems 1960–1967. NDP549.
  Poems 1968–1972. NDP629.
  Sands of the Well. NDP849.
  The Stream and the Sapphire. NDP844.
Harry Levin, *James Joyce.* NDP87.
Li Ch'ing-chao, *Complete Poems.* NDP492.
Li Po, *Selected Poems.* NDP823.
C. Lispector, *Soulstorm.* NDP671.
  The Hour of the Star. NDP733.
  Selected Crónicas. NDP834.
García Lorca, *Five Plays.* NDP232.
  Selected Poems. †NDP114.
  Three Tragedies. NDP52.
Michael McClure, *Simple Eyes.* NDP780.
Carson McCullers, *The Member of the Wedding.* (Playscript)
  NDP153.
X. de Maistre, *Voyage Around My Room.* NDP791.
Stéphane Mallarme,† *Selected Poetry and Prose.*
  NDP529.
Bernadette Mayer, *A Bernadette Mayer Reader.* NDP739.
Thomas Merton, *Asian Journal.* NDP394.
  New Seeds of Contemplation. NDP337.
  Selected Poems. NDP85.
  Thoughts on the East. NDP802.
  The Way of Chuang Tzu. NDP276.
  Zen and the Birds of Appetite. NDP261.
Henri Michaux, *A Barbarian in Asia.* NDP622.
  Selected Writings. NDP264.
Henry Miller, *The Air-Conditioned Nightmare.* NDP302.
  Aller Retour New York. NDP753.
  Big Sur & The Oranges. NDP161.
  The Colossus of Maroussi. NDP75.
  A Devil in Paradise. NDP765.
  Into the Heart of Life. NDP728.
  The Smile at the Foot of the Ladder. NDP386.
Y. Mishima, *Confessions of a Mask.* NDP253.
  Death in Midsummer. NDP215.
Frédéric Mistral, *The Memoirs.* NDP632.

For a complete listing request free catalog from
New Directions, 80 Eighth Avenue, New York 10011   †Bilingual

For a complete listing request free catalog from
New Directions, 80 Eighth Avenue, New York 10011

†Bilingual